© 2009 BluewaterPress, LLC
Saint Augustine, FL

All rights reserved. No part of this book shall be reproduced, stored in a retrieval system, or transmitted by any means without the written permission of the author or the publisher.
All information contained herein was obtained from open sources ranging from most recent Corporate annual reports available at the time of production to respective official company websites.
All content presented in this material has been pre-approved for accuracy at the time of publication by authorized officials of the corresponding featured companies and/or port authorities.
The author nor its publisher assumes no liability for any inaccuracies that may be contained herein.

International Standard Book Number 13: 978-1-60452-036-1
International Standard Book Number 10: 1-60452-036-1
Library of Congress Control Number: 2009935134

BluewaterPress, LLC
52 Tuscan Way Ste 202-309
Saint Augustine, FL 32092
http://www.bluewaterpress.com

This book may be purchased online at http://www.bluewaterpress.com/wings
or through amazon.com

Wings Over America

THE FACT-FILLED GUIDE TO THE MAJOR AND REGIONAL AIRLINES OF THE U.S.A.

MICHAEL COSCIA

INTRODUCTION

In less than half-a-century, air travel has evolved into one of the most popular, quickest, safest, and vital components of transportation available today. Each day, thousands of commercial airliners take to the skies carrying nearly 650 million passengers across the country and throughout the world each year.

The flying public, from the frequent business to the occasional leisure traveler, rely heavily on this booming industry, especially when given a moment's notice. Including our nation's very first passenger service airline in 1926, Western Airlines, which merged with Delta Air Lines in the spring of 1987, hundreds of air carriers have flown out of business. Today, over 300 major, national, and regional airlines—both domestic and international – are flying the world's competitive skies. The United States plays a dominant role in the airline industry where multiple airlines are owned, operated, and based. From the nation's largest airport, Colorado's Denver International Airport, to the nation's busiest, the Hartsfield-Jackson Atlanta International Airport in Georgia, airlines not only maintain their own bustling schedules, but are able to keep up with their passengers as well. Air cargo services, provided by several air cargo companies and mostly all commercial airlines, handle important packages by the hundreds of thousands each day, and manage to get them to their destinations on time. Many companies also offer same-day air services which many people and businesses opt to take advantage of.

As airlines struggle to sustain the building demand of the global industry, a very competitive market has been developed thus far. This strong, tense competition has been beneficial to the consumer by keeping some of the typical "sky-high" air fares low, primarily in markets where competition is most heavy. However, it has proven devastating to the airlines and its employees, especially during times of financial despair in an otherwise struggling economy. Many airlines survive only a few years, while others revitalize with a promising plea as the newer, mainly low-cost, budget startups often pledge. While the largest airlines, primarily legacy carriers, seem to be in control of the market, newer startups continue to form almost as rapidly as others are grounded or merged into other airline companies. Regardless of the ups and downs of the industry, however, it suffices to say that clear skies are ahead for our nation's air carriers. In the times that lie before us, airlines continue to reform and restructure to offer its customers and investors a promising financially successful and profitably stable future, which will eventually lead to future job creation, newer expanded routes, partnerships and alliances, and experimentation of innovative concepts in order to reduce costs; yet hoping to maintain a more lucrative, cost efficient, and expanded global network. The introduction of alternative jet fuel may become available in the near future, significantly easing operating costs and contributing to environmentally-friendly energy needs.

Hub-and-spoking throughout the world, airlines continue to maintain a close watch on each other, beating competitors' fares and matching the lowest "peanuts fares", as some of the growing "no-frills" airlines tend to offer. Many new venture and renowned airlines have a promising outlook on passenger service nowadays. Comfort has been an increasingly key issue, leading to the introduction of additional legroom in the main cabin adding to customer appeal, and newer, state-of-the-art airport facilities continue to break ground. While travelers benefit from these changes, some customary expectations have changed as well. Traditional meal service on almost all airlines flying domestically have been replaced with the latest concept of "buy-on-board" options, and certain amenities we're accustomed to are no longer free of charge, thus introducing a new concept now defined as "debundling". Travelers are now faced with paying additional fees from services ranging from checking baggage at the airline's ticket counter to making reservations through their reservations call center, which will progressively continue to be a growing system-wide trend.

Since this increasingly dynamic, ever-changing industry varies widely in the airline companies' names, ownership information, paint schemes/liveries, services, logos, data, statistics, and marketing brand names, it is sometimes considered a challenge to uphold the correct and current information to ensure the accuracy the information contained within this publication, as it is subject to change at any time; and should be considered a valuable "snapshot-in-time" piece of resourceful literature you as the reader can cherish and appreciate for years to come. Whether you're just enjoying the many photographs and illustrations or reading to familiarize yourself with some of the airline companies to better acquaint you, some perhaps you may be all-too-familiar with, I hope this "fact-filled guide" will serve whatever purposes you seek.

This book is primarily intended to provide a historical, factual, and illustrated overview for airline enthusiasts, future and present employees, frequent travelers, and the vast majority of people in the growing world of aviation, to the nation's fastest- growing major and regional airlines—the wings over America.

Acknowledgments

The author would like to thank the following numerous amounts of wonderful people, organizations, and facilities for gracious assistance with various levels of support:

Alberto and Emma Coscia
Professor Joe Clark: Department of Aeronautical Science
    Embry-Riddle Aeronautical University, Daytona Beach, FL
Aviation Partners Boeing, Seattle, WA
David A. Wegman: Greater Orlando Aviation Authority,
    Orlando International Airport, Orlando, FL
Dr. Richard C. Sanzenbacher: Department of Humanities and Social Sciences,
    Embry-Riddle Aeronautical University, Daytona Beach, FL
Dr. Lynn Koller, Department of Humanities and Social Sciences,
    Embry-Riddle Aeronautical University, Daytona Beach, FL
Professor Thomas Vickers, Department of Humanities and Social Sciences,
    Embry-Riddle Aeronautical University, Daytona Beach, FL
International Air Transportation Association
International Civil Aviation Organization
Denver International Airport
Seattle-Tacoma International Airport
Fort Lauderdale-Hollywood International Airport
Ted Stevens Anchorage International Airport
Hartsfield-Jackson Atlanta International Airport
David G. Coscia
Steven Lucas
Chad D. Stillwagon
Dan Nye
Amy Bley
Kathy Gleason
Air Wisconsin Airlines Corporation, Inc.
AirTran Airways, Inc.
Alaska Airlines, Inc.
Allegiant Air, Inc.
American Airlines, Inc.
Atlantic Southeast Airlines, Inc.
Cape Air, Inc.
Colgan Air, Inc.
Comair, Inc.
CommutAir / Champlain Enterprises, Inc.
Compass Airlines, Inc.
Continental Airlines, Inc.
Delta Air Lines, Inc.
ExpressJet Airlines, Inc.
Frontier Airlines, Inc.
Frontier Flying Service, Inc.
GoJet Airlines, Inc.
Great Lakes Airlines, Inc.

Hawaiian Airlines, Inc.
Horizon Air, Inc.
JetBlue Airways, Inc.
Lynx Aviation, Inc.
Mesa Air Group, Inc.
Mesaba Airlines, Inc.
Midwest Airlines, Inc.
Peninsula Airways, Inc.
Pinnacle Airlines, Inc.
Republic Airways, Inc.
SkyWest Airlines, Inc.
Southwest Airlines, Co.
Spirit Airlines, Inc.
Sun Country Airlines, Inc.
Trans States Airlines, Inc.
United Airlines, Inc.
US Airways, Inc.
USA3000 Airlines, Inc.
Virgin America, Inc.
Heidi Bausch
Jarek Beem
Carlo Bertolini
Bill Boyer
Michael Brophy
Michelle Brown
Todd Burke
Maggie Clark
Wendy Clements
Patricia Condon
Kelly Cripe
Daniel Cuellar
Annette Daly
Jordan Decker
Chris Fink
Lynn Flaquer
Brian Gillman
Lori Goodman
Derek Hanna
Michelle Haynes
Andrea Huguely
Michael Husson
Sharon Jones
Cory Kohler

Jeff Kovick
Bill Lehman
Janis Logue
Abby Lunardini
Robert Long
Brian Lusk
David Messing
Michelle Moreton
Kristy Nicholas
Benjamin F. Oxley
Misty Pinson
Stephanie Powell
Jeff Pugh
Mike Rose
Dianna M. Sinicrope
Marissa Snow
Tyri Squyres
Ron Suttell
Monica Taylor
Robin Urbanski
Keoni Wagner
Kathy Weishaar
Christopher White
Joe Williams

TABLE OF CONTENTS

Air Wisconsin Airlines	76
AirTran Airways	6
Alaska Airlines	10
Allegiant Air	14
American Airlines	18
American Connection	76
American Eagle	76
Atlantic Southeast Airlines (ASA)	77

Cape Air	77
Chautauqua Airlines	77
Colgan Air	78
Comair	78
CommutAir	78
Compass Airlines	79
Continental Airlines	22
Continental Connection	79
Continental Express	79

Delta Air Lines	26
Delta Connection	80
Delta Shuttle	80

Era Aviation	80
ExpressJet Airlines	81

Freedom Airlines	81
Frontier Airlines	30
Frontier Alaska	81

go!	82
go! Express	82
GoJet Airlines	82
Great Lakes Airlines	83
Gulfstream International	83

Hageland Aviation	83
Hawaiian Airlines	34
Horizon Air	84

Island Air	84

JetBlue Airways	38

Lynx Aviation	84

Mesa Airlines	85
Mesaba Airlines	85
Midwest Airlines	42
Midwest Connect	85
Mokulele Airlines	86

Peninsula Airways (PenAir)	86
Piedmont Airlines	86
Pinnacle Airlines	87
PSA Airlines	87

Republic Airlines	87

Shuttle America	88
SkyWest Airlines	88
Southwest Airlines	46
Spirit Airlines	50
Sun Country Airlines	54

Trans States Airlines	88

United Airlines	58
United Express	89
US Airways	62
US Airways Express	89
US Airways Shuttle	89
USA3000 Airlines	66

Virgin America	70

List of U.S. Airport Codes	90
Index	97

Wings Over America

Boeing 717-200

AIRTRAN AIRWAYS

Serving as the world's largest operator of the Boeing 717, AirTran Airways is known to be a combination of several former defunct airline employees who joined together to form a strategic plan to develop a single low-cost, high-frequency airline. In 1992, the predecessor airline, ValuJet Airlines, was founded by airline industry veterans, including an executive group from the former Atlanta-based Southern Airways, including pilots, mechanics, and flight attendants from Eastern Air Lines, which ceased operations on January 18, 1991.

Created to fill the void at Hartsfield-Atlanta Jackson International Airport after Eastern's demise, ValuJet launched operations with two former Delta Air Lines McDonnell-Douglas DC9 aircraft, when the first scheduled passenger flight occurred on October 26, 1993 from Atlanta to Tampa. In the spring of 1994, barely eight months of service between Atlanta and three Florida cities, the airline went public by listing its stock on the NASDAQ and trading under the ticker symbol "VJET."

In late 1995, after two years of service the public's air transportation needs, the airline placed an order with the McDonnell-Douglas Corporation to be the launch customer for the MD-95 aircraft—now known as the Boeing 717. Serving as the launch customer meant the airline would have much input into the overall design of the aircraft, and ValuJet was the youngest airline to serve as a lunch customer for such aircraft type. At the end of 1995, the airline who was well known for carrying its very own cartoon airplane logo known as "critter", was named as the top company in the famed *Georgia 100* as published by the *Atlanta Journal-Constitution*, and posted high margins with a $67 million net profit on revenues exceeding $367 million. The publicly-traded airline's stock increased in value on a seemingly weekly basis.

The original AirTran Airways, a Boeing 737 operator with service to and from Orlando, Florida was founded by AirTran Corporation; the holding company of Minneapolis-based Mesaba Airlines, operating as a Northwest Airlink carrier with hubs existing in the Twin Cities and Detroit. In 1994, AirTran Holdings purchased a startup 737 operator, Conquest Sun, in which similar to ValuJet being an airline started by former Eastern Air Lines employees; and renamed the airline AirTran Airways. The original AirTran Airways moved its headquarters to Orlando, and grew its fleet to 11 Boeing 737 aircraft serving 24 cities in the Eastern and Midwestern U.S. providing low fare leisure travel to and from the Central Florida resort destination. In 1995, AirTran Airways was separated from Mesaba and formed its own independent holding company—Airways Corporation, based in Orlando.

On July 10, 1997 ValuJet, Inc. announced plans to acquire Airways Corporation, and the deal was scheduled to finalize on November 17, 1997. In that same year, AirTran began assigning seats on all of its flights, compared to its previous first-come, first-served seating strategy; a common practice with high-frequency, low-cost carriers. The following month, the airline added business class seats on every flight—highly uncommon among low-cost carriers. The former route system to and from Orlando operated by AirTran were terminated following the merger with ValuJet Airlines to begin focus on the airline's new hub in Atlanta. In March 1998, AirTran launched its frequent flyer program, A+ Rewards. *Entrepreneur Magazine* presented the airline its 1998 award for "Best Domestic Low-Fare Airline" in June of that year; also winning this particular award in 2001, 2002, 2004, and 2005. In July 1998, AirTran reported its first profitable fiscal quarter since early 1996 gaining increasingly public interest. On September 24, 1997 ValuJet Airlines changed its

AIRTRAN AIRWAYS

name to AirTran Airlines. For a brief period, the two holding companies, even though they had not yet merged, operated two separate airlines with slightly similar names — AirTran *Airlines* and AirTran *Airways*. ValuJet, Inc. operated AirTran Airlines with their hub in Atlanta, and Airways, Inc. operated AirTran Airways with its hub in Orlando. Finally, on November 17, 1997 ValuJet, Inc. acquired Airways, Inc., and renamed the parent company AirTran Holdings, Inc. In the summer of 1998, the two airlines merged onto the same FAA certificate, and the AirTran Airways name remained. While the existing hub persisted in Atlanta, the headquarters of the new entity was consolidated in Orlando on January 28, 1998.

On September 24, 1999, the airline took delivery of the Boeing 717, many of which were acquired from former Trans World Airlines (TWA), following its demise in 2001. The first of its kind entered service on October 12, 1999. On December 12, 2000 AirTran launched services from Atlanta to its first international destination, Grand Bahama Island. On July 1, 2003, the carrier placed orders for 100 Boeing 737 aircraft which took delivery in June 2004. The airline then changed its livery to a fresh, more modern look, with white replacing the former tan color; retaining its teal colored tailfin that bears its large, white, bold, lowercase "a" logo. In October 2003, the airline initiated service to Washington D.C.'s Reagan National Airport and to San Francisco the following month. In February 2005, it became the first commercial airline to offer *XM Satellite Radio* as in-flight entertainment on board all its aircraft in both business class and coach. In November 2006, the airline forged a marketing partnership with Frontier Airlines, allowing frequent flyers to earn airline miles in either AirTran's A+ Rewards, or Frontier's EarlyReturns frequent flyer program. This is known as reciprocal earning (as opposed to reciprocal redemption). In addition, the airlines will refer customers to each other when appropriate since no existing interline agreements with other airlines exist. On January 5, 2004 AirTran's last Douglas DC-9 retired from service, leaving it with a fleet of more than 70 Boeing 717 aircraft. Throughout the years, the airline has grown its fleet of aircraft and maintains two types from Boeing to help streamline maintenance operations and maintain a cost effective pricing and operational structure. AirTran Airways took delivery of the last Boeing 717 to roll off the assembly line at the aircraft manufacturer's Long Beach, California facility in May 2006. The airline became the first major U.S. carrier to offer Wi-fi on every flight in 2009, while operating 750 daily flights; including over 270 daily departures from its primary hub at the world's busiest airport – the Hartsfield-Jackson Atlanta International Airport in Georgia.

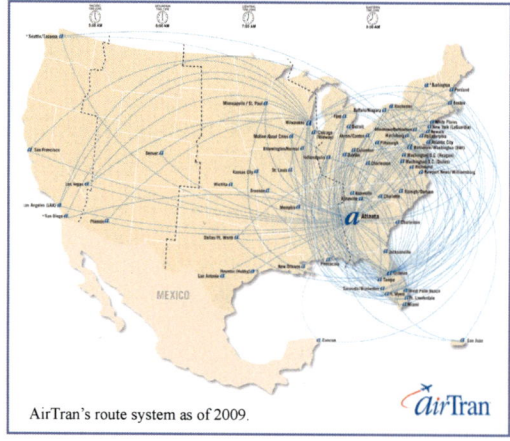

AirTran's route system as of 2009.

AIRTRAN AIRWAYS

Boeing 737-700

Boeing 737-700

Facts & Figures

Founded	1994 (as Conquest Sun Airlines)
Callsign	"CITRUS"
IATA designator	FL
IATA accounting	332
ICAO designator	TRS
Frequent flyer program	A+ Rewards
Fleet count	136

(86) B717-200, (50) B737-700 (with 63 on order by 2012)

Total destinations	56
Total countries served	2
Parent company	AirTran Holdings: NYSE: AAI
Headquarters	Orlando, FL
In-flight magazine	GO
Member lounge	N/A
Primary hub(s)	Atlanta
Secondary hub(s)	Orlando and Baltimore/Washington Int'l
Subsidiaries	N/A
Global Alliance	N/A
Approximate number of employees	8,500
Website	airtran.com
Toll-free reservations	1-800-247-8726
Route structure	Hub-and-spoke
Reservations computer system	SkySpeed
Reservations call center locations	Atlanta, Savannah, and Carrolton, GA
Boeing customer code	BD

9

Boeing 737-800

ALASKA AIRLINES

Since deregulation, Seattle-based Alaska Airlines has historically been one of the largest carriers on the United States' west coast as well as to and within the State of Alaska, with strong presences in the Pacific Northwest—primarily Seattle, Portland, the San Francisco Bay Area, and the Los Angeles Metropolitan area; where it serves all five LA-area and three Bay Area major airports. The airline, through sound business and consistent marketing strategies, grew to dominate the West Coast and West Coast to Alaska markets over the last 25 years, claiming their position wasn't inherited, but earned through "beating the competition".

The nation's seventh largest airline traces its roots to 1932 as McGee Airways, owned by Linious "Mac" McGee. The Territory of Alaska, considered a land of opportunity by many, inspired McGee; who at the time was running a fur-trading business. His purchase of a single-engine, three-passenger Stinson airplane led to the start of McGee Airways linking Anchorage and Bristol Bay. McGee Airways merged with Star Air Service in 1934, creating the largest airline in Alaska with more than 20 aircraft. Mergers and acquisitions produced changes in the name and saw business expand throughout the territory. As of 1942, the airline was known as Alaska Star Airlines after takeovers of other small airlines gave the airline a large share of the services in Alaska.

An evolution in names ended in 1944 with the final selection of its present name—Alaska Airlines. The carrier then moved its corporate headquarters from Anchorage to Paine Field in Everett, WA; in order to consolidate all of its major base operations, including administrative and executive offices, stores, shops, and maintenance base all in one location; and was coincidentally a less costly alternative. Alaska's largest airline has made its mark in aviation history for over 75 years. In 1951, it was the first airline to fly over the North Pole in a DC-4 and the first air transport carrier to offer in-flight movies. In 1961, Alaska set a new Los Angeles to Seattle speed record with their very first jet, the Convair 880. In 1964, the carrier introduced a nonstop route from Seattle to Anchorage.

In 1970, Alaska Airlines pioneered charter flight tours to Russia from the West Coast and was also the first to introduce heads-up guidance technology, proclaimed the "fog-buster" on commercial airliners by 1989. In 1972, nearing the end of the airline's troubled financial past, Alaska introduced a new paint scheme to replace the "Golden Nugget" theme with four images of Alaska: a sourdough prospector, a totem pole, Russian Orthodox church domes, and an Eskimo. The livery was standardized in 1978 unveiling a larger-than-life, smiling, friendly portrait of a Native Alaskan Eskimo emblazoned on each aircraft's tail fin; a true symbol of the airline's rich Alaskan heritage. This newly enhanced image grew to symbolize the warm yet unique spirit of our 49th state, as well as the prominent mainstay of the proud livery for the growing carrier. The new image brought forth their former slogan "Fly with a Happy Face", which was introduced as part of their widespread marketing campaign scheme as well as its corporate slogan.

In 1985, Alaska Airlines' holding company, Alaska Air Group, was formed along with the acquisition of Horizon Air, whose partnership commenced in 1986 and currently operates as the carrier's wholly owned sister airline, and Jet America Airlines in 1987. Horizon Air's route system is closely integrated into Alaska's operations, with Alaska and Horizon sharing many routes in their combined expansive network. It wasn't until the spring of 1990 when Alaska Airlines unveiled its present paint scheme and logo. Undoubtedly, the carrier retained the smiling face image, and replaced its interior with upholstery that reflects Native American designs from Alaska, the Southwest, and Mexico. With the growing success of low-cost / low-fare carriers, the airline industry changed in fundamental ways in the 1990s. Streamlining its cost structure and increasing aircraft utilization, Alaska Airlines reshaped itself faster and more comprehensively than any carrier, all while maintaining a competitive advantage in customer service. When coupled with an unmatched market presence on the West Coast, the recipe added up to record passenger traffic and greater profitability.

The current decade has seen Alaska Airlines expand its growing network not only throughout Alaska, but across the lower 48 to Boston, Chicago, Dallas, Denver, Miami, Newark, Orlando, Washington, D.C., and Minneapolis. The airline also has crossed the Pacific with much-heralded service that began in 2007 to the Hawaiian Islands and added more destinations in Mexico. The transition from a combination of older Boeing 737-200s and McDonnell Douglas MD-82 and MD-83s, which all retired out of service by the end of 2008, to an expanded, all Boeing 737 fleet meant greater fuel savings and other efficiencies and respect for the environment.

In 2006, the airline launched its buy on board meal program, *Northern Bites*, offerered on most flights in coach class over three hours in length. and various "Picnic Packs" for coach class on all flights. Inflight Wi-Fi broadband wireless internet access was launched in 2009, providing the growing airline with newer in-flight services to coincide with the reality of the changing times ahead.

Background photo: Tail and blended winglets of Alaska Airlines' "Starliner 75" aircraft, unveiled with a special livery to commemorate the Company's 75th anniversary in 2007.

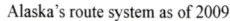

Alaska's route system as of 2009.

• Alaska Airlines Cities
◦ Cities Jointly Served by Alaska Airlines and Horizon Air
• Horizon Air Cities

Alaska Airlines' loyalty program, Mileage Plan, includes partnership agreements with Air France, American Airlines, British Airways, Cathay Pacific, Continental Airlines, Delta Air Lines, Era Aviation, Frontier Alaska, Horizon Air, KLM, Korean Air, LAN, Mokulele Airlines, PenAir, and Qantas.

In addition to Alaska Airlines Board Room locations in Anchorage, Seattle, Portland, Los Angeles, Vancouver, and San Francisco, members have access to 51 affiliate lounges worldwide through special agreements with other airlines.

ALASKA AIRLINES

Alaska's Eskimo with Hawaiian lei

Boeing 737-400, *"Spirit of Disneyland"* (N784AS)

Facts & Figures

Founded.............................	1932 (McGee Airways)
Callsign.............................	"ALASKA"
IATA designator.................	AS
IATA accounting................	027
ICAO designator................	ASA
Frequent flyer program......	Mileage Plan
Fleet count........................	116

(28) B737-400, (1) B737-400F, (5) B737-400C, (19) B737-700, (50) B737-800, (12) B737-900

Total destinations..............	61
Total countries served.......	3
Parent company................	Alaska Air Group : NYSE: ALK
Headquarters....................	SeaTac, WA
In-flight magazine.............	*Alaska Airlines Magazine*
Member lounge.................	Board Room
Primary hub(s)..................	Seattle/Tacoma
Secondary hub(s)..............	Anchorage, Portland, Los Angeles
Sister carrier.....................	Horizon Air
Global Alliance..................	N/A
Approximate number of employees...	13,550
Website.............................	alaskaair.com
Toll-free reservations........	1-800-426-0333
Route structure.................	Hub-and-spoke
Reservations computer system.........	SABRE
Reservations call center locations......	Boise, Seattle, and Tempe, AZ
Boeing customer code......................	90

13

McDonnell-Douglas MD-83

Allegiant Air, a wholly owned subsidiary of Allegiant Travel Company, was founded in 1997 in Fresno, California and began scheduled passenger service in November 1998 flying a single McDonnell-Douglas DC-9 aircraft. The company's original business model was unsuccessful, and it entered Chapter 11 bankruptcy in 2000. In June 2001, Maurice J. Gallagher, Jr., Allegiant's major creditor, gained control of the company; ultimately restructuring the airline into a low-cost carrier and moving its headquarters and operations to Las Vegas.

In March 2002, Allegiant successfully exited bankruptcy on the foundation of a long-term contract with Harrah's Entertainment, Inc. to provide charter services to its casinos in the Nevada cities of Laughlin and Reno, allowing the airline to acquire its first MD-80 aircraft. Together with chief financial officer Andrew Levy and managing director Ponder Harrison, Gallagher spent the period from 2002 through 2004 developing the basics of Allegiant's scheduled service business model. By 2004, Allegiant flew from 13 small cities to Las Vegas offering bundled air and hotel vacation packages. Since that time, Allegiant has successfully extended its business model to Florida (Orlando in 2005, St. Petersburg in 2006, and Fort Lauderdale in 2007), and western U.S. cties including Phoenix in 2007 and Los Angeles in 2009. Along the way, Allegiant's parent company, Allegiant Travel Company, successfully completed an initial public offering in December 2006 and became listed on the NASDAQ under ticker symbol "ALGT".

Today, Allegiant continues its focus on the previously underserved niche of flying leisure travelers in smaller communities to significantly larger leisure destinations, generally from airports that have limited or even no prior service. Allegiant is considered to be led by a team of successful industry veterans who take the proven attributes of the low-cost airline business model and have creatively adapted them to best address the company's targeted leisure clientele and focus destinations.

As of June, 2009, the airline operates a fleet of 43 McDonnell-Douglas MD-80 series jet aircraft, employs more than 1,600 personnel, and maintains bases in six focus cities: Las Vegas McCarran International Airport, Orlando Sanford International Airport, St. Petersburg-Clearwater International Airport, Los Angeles International Airport, Phoenix-Mesa Gateway Airport and Fort Lauderdale-Hollywood International Airport. Allegiant Air also maintains a seventh operational base at Bellingham International Airport in Washington State, providing nonstop scheduled service to/from more than 70 U.S. cities. In addition to its scheduled service, the airline continues to offer charter service throughout the U.S., Mexico, the Caribbean, and Canada. The carrier's charter customers include Harrah's Entertainment, several athletic organizations, film production companies, corporations, and the US Department of Defense. In addition, the company has recently inaugurated charter service to Cuba on behalf of several sponsoring organizations.

Some of the many destinations Allegiant serves, as of June, 2009, are: Allentown/Lehigh Valley, PA; Appleton/Green Bay, WI; Bangor, ME; Bellingham, WA; Billings, MT; Bismarck, ND; Bozeman, MT; Casper, WY; Cedar Rapids, IA; Chattanooga, TN; Colorado Springs, CO; Columbia, SC; Des Moines, IA; Duluth/Superior, MN; Elmira-Corning, NY; Eugene, OR; Fargo, ND; Fort Collins/Loveland, CO; Fort Lauderdale, FL; Fort Wayne, IN; Fresno, CA; Grand Forks, ND; Grand Island, NE; Grand Junction, CO; Grand Rapids, MI; Great Falls, MT; Greensboro, NC; Greenville/Spartanburg, SC; Hagerstown, MD; Huntington, WV;

ALLEGIANT AIR

Idaho Falls, ID; Kalispell, MT.; Knoxville, TN; Laredo, TX; Las Vegas, NV; Lexington, KY; Los Angeles, CA; McAllen, TX; Medford, OR; Missoula, MT; Monterey, CA, Myrtle Beach, SC; Fayetteville, AR - Northwest Arkansas Regional; Oakland, CA; Orlando-Sanford, FL; Owensboro, KY; Palm Springs, CA; Pasco, WA; Peoria, IL; Phoenix-Mesa, AZ; Plattsburgh, NY; Punta Gorda/Southwest Florida Coast, FL; Rapid City, SD; Redmond/Bend, OR; Roanoke, VA; Rochester, MN; Rockford, IL; San Diego, CA; Santa Barbara, CA; Santa Maria, CA; Shreveport, LA; Sioux Falls, SD; South Bend, IN; Springfield, MO; Stockton, CA; Toledo, OH; Tri-Cities, TN; Wichita, KS; Wilmington, NC; and Youngstown, OH.

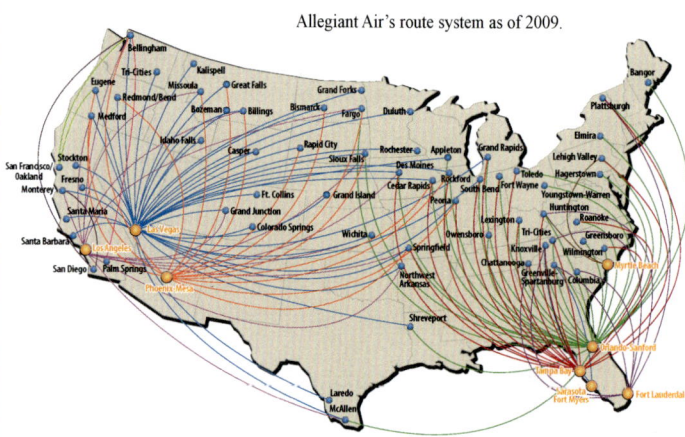
Allegiant Air's route system as of 2009.

Maury Gallagher, President and CEO of Allegiant Air, and crew.

16

ALLEGIANT AIR

McDonnell-Douglas MD-88

McDonnell-Douglas MD-88 at Ft. Collins-Loveland Municipal Airport, Colorado

Facts & Figures

Founded	1997
Callsign	"ALLEGIANT"
IATA designator	G4
IATA accounting	268
ICAO designator	AAY
Frequent flyer program	N/A
Fleet count	43

(8) MD-82, (25) MD-83, (4) MD-87, (6) MD-88

Total destinations	71
Total countries served	1
Parent company	Allegiant Travel Co.: NASDAQ: ALGT
Headquarters	Las Vegas, NV
In-flight magazine	*Sunseeker*
Member lounge	N/A
Focus cities	LAS, SFB, PIE, FLL, IWA, LAX and BLI
Subsidiaries	Allegiant Vacations
Global Alliance	N/A
Approximate number of employees	1,600
Website	allegiantair.com
Reservations	(702) 505-8888
Route structure	Point-to-point
Reservations computer system	Allegiant Information Systems
Reservations call center locations	Las Vegas

17

AmericanAirlines®

Boeing 767-300ER

AMERICAN AIRLINES

America's flagship carrier has grown to be one of the world's largest, successful, and most time-honored airlines in existence. The main subsidiary of Texas-based AMR Corporation can track its origin to the morning of April 15, 1926 when Charles A. Lindbergh, a young aviator and chief pilot for Robertson Aircraft Corporation, flew a bag of mail on board a DH-4 bi-plane from Chicago to St. Louis. The corporation and approximately 85 other small aviation companies joined forces in 1929 and 1930 to form The Aviation Corporation which eventually formed American Airways, the immediate forerunner of today's American Airlines.

In 1933, American began operating the 18-passenger Curtiss Condor, providing the first appearance of flight attendants for the soon-to-be globally recognized Company. The airline reorganized on April 11, 1934 and became American Airlines, Inc., which on June 25, 1936, flew the world's first commercial flight, on a Douglas DC-3, from Chicago to New York. By the end of the decade, American was the nation's number one domestic air carrier in terms of revenue passenger miles. On February 16, 1939, just five years after its inaugural scheduled flight, American carried its one-millionth passenger. The introduction of international service occurred June 1941, with service from New York to Toronto, Canada.

Already in high gear, the airline established its Tulsa, Oklahoma maintenance and engineering base in 1946. Less than one year later, the DC-6 entered service, equipped with a fully pressurized cabin offering sleeper service, "Skysleeper," between New York and Los Angeles via Chicago and Dallas, with additional stopovers. Entering the jet age, American became the first airline to offer coast-to-coast all-jet service on Boeing 707s, which began flying in American's colors on January 25, 1959. At the end of 1959 and into the early 1960s, American, teaming up with IBM, introduced and implemented SABRE (Semi-Automated Business Research Environment), the largest, non-military, electronic data processing system for business use. Operations at Chicago's O'Hare International Airport originated in 1962, expanding the carrier's service in the Midwest. By 1964, the SABRE network extended from Canada to Mexico and across the country. It became the largest real-time data processing system, second only to the U.S. Government's SAGE system. That same year, the Boeing 727 was added to the growing fleet. The McDonnell-Douglas DC-10 made its first scheduled flight in August, 1971, in which the airline was the first to order.

Gaining Caribbean routes through a merger with Trans-Caribbean Airways in 1970, the airline began flying to Puerto Rico, the U.S. Virgin Islands, Haiti, Curacao, and Aruba in March 1971. Later, several more Caribbean routes followed, and to better serve destinations in that market, the Airbus A300-600ER twin-aisle service was introduced to American in 1988. On June 11, 1981, American established its first hub at Dallas/Fort Worth International Airport in Texas, just one year after retiring the 707 from service. The airline's second hub at Chicago/O'Hare opened in 1982. In 1984, American's vast network of regional commuter service was introduced as American Eagle, which currently serves as the carrier's main regional partner and one of the world's largest regional airline systems, connecting passengers from small airport communities to large cities to and from the American Airlines mainline system, employing over 12,000 personnel. It was during this era that the Company unveiled its popular marketing slogan, "Something Special in the Air", which gained popular attention and marketing appeal throughout the global industry. By 1989, while opening its seventh hub at Miami International

AMERICAN AIRLINES

Airport on September 13, 1989, American was rated one of the nation's largest airlines with over 55,000 employees. The airline's second successful merger with Orange County, California based AirCal in July, 1987, helped expand the airline's West Coast markets which included a high-frequency network within California and throughout the Pacific Northwest. The summer of 1990 marked a significant milestone for the inauguration of the airline giant's Latin American route network. American obtained rights to fly to 20 Central and South American gateways which were acquired by the financially stricken Miami-based Eastern Air Lines, which ceased operations in January of 1991. The airline, along with four others, joined the **one**world global alliance which launched February 1, 1999. The merger between American Airlines and St. Louis, Missouri-based Trans World Airlines (TWA), was finalized in April 2001.

From the time C.R. Smith, the airline's longtime president and aviation pioneer, assumed his role in 1934 to today, American Airlines serves as one of the world's largest airlines, contributing more than $150 billion per year to the U.S. economy. American Airlines and its regional airlines affiliates, American Eagle and AmericanConnection, serve 250 cities in over 40 countries with more than 3,400 daily flights.

American's 2009 domestic destinations. (**U.S. cities not shown:** Bangor, ME; Boston, MA; Providence, RI; Hartford/Springfield, CT; and New York's JFK and La Guardia Airports.)

"History takes flight": The American Airlines C.R. Smith Museum, located just south of Dallas/Fort Worth International Airport, is a one-of-a-kind adventure into the world of commercial aviation and a tribute to the history of American Airlines. The museum opened its doors in July 1993, and is dedicated to past and present American Airlines employees. The museum, considered *"window-seat look at the world of flight"*, is a non-profit organization funded by the C.R. Smith Aviation Museum Foundation and emphasizes learning through audible, visual, and hands-on displays.

American Airlines' frequent flyer program, AAdvantage, was established in 1981, which consists of over 60 million members.

With over 38 locations worldwide, American Airlines' Admirals Club has served as the airline's premier member lounge at select airports since its first location opened its doors in 1939 at New York's La Guardia Airport.

AMERICAN AIRLINES

McDonnell-Douglas MD-83, *"Super 80"*

Boeing 777-200ER

Facts & Figures

Founded	1930 (American Airways)
Callsign	"AMERICAN"
IATA designator	AA
IATA accounting	001
ICAO designator	AAL
Frequent flyer program	AAdvantage
Fleet count	616 (+260 orders, 58 purchase rights)

(23) A300-605R, (79) B737-800 (+87 orders), (124) B757-223 (+124 orders), (15) B767-233ER, (58) B767-323ER, (47) B777-200ER (+7 orders), (0) B787-9 (+42 orders, 58 purchase rights), (271) MD-80

Total destinations	250
Total countries served	40
Parent company	AMR Corporation : NYSE: AMR
Headquarters	Fort Worth, TX
In-flight magazine	*American Way*, *Celebrated Living*, and *Nexos*
Member lounge	Admirals Club
Primary hub(s)	Dallas/Ft. Worth, Chicago/O'Hare, St. Louis, Miami, and San Juan.
Secondary hub(s)	JFK, LGA, BOS, and LAX
Regional carrier	American Eagle
Brands	American Connection
Global Alliance	one*world*
Approximate number of employees	82,000
Website	aa.com
Toll-free reservations	1-800-433-7300
Route structure	Hub-and-spoke
Reservations computer system	SABRE
Reservations call center locations	Tucson, Cary, NC, and Hartford, CT
Boeing customer code	23

21

Continental Airlines

Boeing 777-200

CONTINENTAL AIRLINES

Similar to the historical background of most experienced airlines that survived from the 1930s, the origin of Continental Airlines can be traced to that historic era as Varney Speed Lines, named after one of its original owners, Walter T. Varney, also a founder of United Airlines, which operated as a small domestic airmail contracted carrier whose inaugural flight on July 15, 1934 took it from El Paso, Texas to Pueblo, Colorado. The pilot, Jess E. Hart, carried 100 letters on that solo flight through the skies of the American Southwest.

Robert F. Six, who joined Varney's management team in 1937, changed the airline's name to Continental Airlines on July 8 of that year, and unveiled a new logo of the image of a Native American, symbolizing its rich Southwestern heritage. In 1940, air hostesses were introduced to serve passengers on board Continental's fleet of Convair 240, 340 and DC-3 aircraft by the early 1950s. Pioneer Airlines was added as a merger partner in 1951, expanding its small route network throughout the Southwest and Texas. When Houston was added to Continental's fast developing route system in 1951, the airline placed purchases for a variety of modern aircraft such as the Boeing 720, which replaced the time-honored and well served fleet of Douglas DC-3s. In 1957, the airline's traditional "Gold Carpet Service" began. The airline has since been related with the notoriously favorable color.

In the spring of 1959, the airline took delivery of its first Boeing 707 and was used to fly their nonstop routes between Chicago and Los Angeles. As the 1960s approached, the airline added routes from Los Angeles to Houston, and between Houston and Phoenix and five Texas cities. Service was then expanded shortly after from Denver to Portland, Seattle, and New Orleans. Delivered in 1972, its first McDonnell-Douglas DC-10 featured its now retired gold, orange, and red livery; with its golden tails bearing their famous red logo, at first black, which was nicknamed the "meatball" by several of the airline's employees and airline enthusiasts. By 1979, DC-10 service was scheduled to fly several Pacific routes including Sydney, Australia from Los Angeles; via Honolulu and Fiji.

In 1982, entering a period of fierce competition and fare wars due to deregulation, the airline merged with Texas International Airlines. Continental, already held by Houston-based Texas Air Corporation, suffered severe losses which led the Company into Chapter 11 bankruptcy in 1983 only to emerge in 1986. In the late 1980s, the legacy carrier acquired four of the nation's profitable, high-frequency, low-cost airlines. Beginning with the Denver's original Frontier Airlines in 1986, Continental reached agreements to buy out assets with other airlines such as New York Air and Newark-based PEOPLExpress in 1987, creating the third-largest U.S. airline, and fifth largest airline in the world. Following the demise of Eastern Air Lines, once a model carrier and Continental's joint partner in 1991, the airline's primitive computerized network system, SystemOne, and their partnership in the frequent flyer program, OnePass, integrated into Continental.

Following its expansion at Cleveland Hopkins International Airport, which became the airline's third largest hub following Houston and Newark, the airline unveiled its current blue and gray livery reflecting the airline's global network, also retaining its admirable gold highlights including a stripe that extends the entire length of each of its 350-plus aircraft. For nearly forty years, the airline operated an extensive hub at the former Denver Stapleton Airport when plans called for the closure of the now largest airport in the United States, following it's renovation in

CONTINENTAL AIRLINES

1995, as it was renamed Denver International Airport (D.I.A.). In 1999, the first nonstop flight from Houston to Asia was announced with Continental's inaugural flight from the Texas hub to Tokyo, Japan's Narita International Airport.

Having celebrated its 75th anniversary in 2009, the airline has consistently earned awards and critical acclaim for both its operation and corporate culture. For six consecutive years, *FORTUNE* Magazine had named Continental Airlines the "Number One World's Most Admired Airline" on its 2009 list of "World's Most Admired Companies". Continental, together with Continental Micronesia, Continental Express, and Continental Connection, operated by a variety of regional airlines, operates more than 2,750 daily departures throughout its vast system and employs over 42,000 employees worldwide.

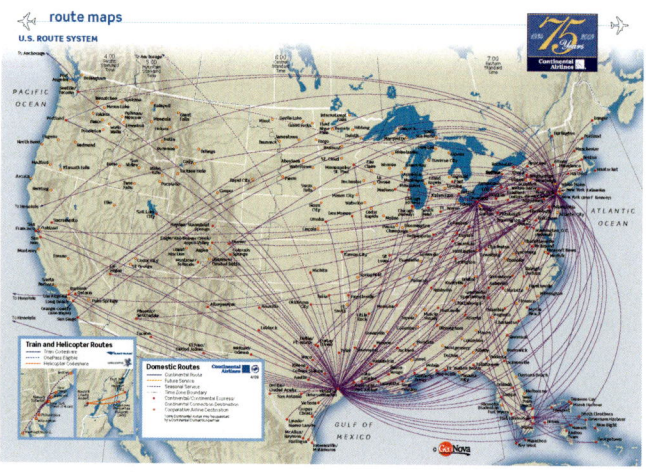

Continental Airlines' domestic route system as of 2009.

Continental magazine is the award-winning inflight magazine for Continental Airlines and their successful, discerning travelers.

Nearing its 30th location at select airports, Continental's Presidents Club has been caters to their paid members, OnePass top-tier, first class, and select BusinessFirst passengers.

Launched in October, 1992, the airline's premium cabin offers the latest in comfort appeal, including modern technology such as electronic "one touch" controls and entertainment device connectivity. In 2009 plans include to fit each BusinessFirst cabin environment with 180 degree reclining sleeper seats equipped with six way adjustable head rests. Available only on 757, 767, and future widebody aircraft.

24

CONTINENTAL AIRLINES

Boeing 737-800

Boeing 757-200

Facts & Figures

Founded	1934 (as Varney Speed Lines)
Callsign	"CONTINENTAL"
IATA designator	CO
IATA accounting	005
ICAO designator	CAL
Frequent flyer program	OnePass
Fleet count	352 (+ 70 orders)

(23) 737-300, (42) 737-500, (36) 737-700, (116) 737-800 (+5 orders), (12) 737-900, (19) 737-900ER (+28 orders), (41) 757-200, (17) 757-300, (10) 767-200ER, (16) 767-400ER, (20) 777-200 (+8 orders), (0) 787-800 (+8 orders), (0) 787-900 (+17 orders)

Total destinations	265
Total countries served	49
Parent company	Continental Airlines, Inc. : NYSE: CAL
Headquarters	Houston, TX
In-flight magazine	*Continental* magazine
Member lounge	Presidents Club
Primary hub(s)	Cleveland, Newark, and Houston (IAH)
Secondary hub(s)	Guam (operated by Continental Micronesia)
Subsidiaries	Continental Micronesia
Brands	Continental Connection, Continental Express
Global Alliance	Star Alliance (October 25, 2009)
Approximate number of employees	42,605
Website	continental.com
Toll-free reservations	1-800-525-0280
Route structure	Hub-and-spoke
Reservations computer system	EZR
Reservations call center locations	Houston, Tampa, and Salt Lake City
Boeing Customer Code	24

25

Boeing 777-200LR

DELTA AIR LINES

After a very successful merger announced in 2008 with Northwest Airlines, Atlanta-based Delta Air Lines prides itself in being the world's largest airline, serving over 370 destinations worldwide and operating a fleet of over 1,000 aircraft. Pioneers of hub-and-spoke, the major carrier traces its roots to 1928, when a group of Monroe, Louisiana businessmen, along with C.E. Woolman, an agricultural engineer and aviation enthusiast, and entrepreneurs of the world's first aerial crop dusting organization, Huff Daland Dusters, created a powerful weapon to defeat a significant insect problem that was destroying the precious cotton fields along the Mississippi River Delta Region. Spraying this insecticide from the air became a promising method of destroying the pesky pest, well known as the boll weevil.

As a result of this venture, Delta Air Corporation was formed in 1928, utilizing five-passenger, single-engine aircraft with a cruising speed of 90 miles per hour. Passenger service was introduced on June 17, 1929, flying routes between Dallas, Texas, and Jackson, Mississippi via Shreveport and Monroe, Louisiana. The route that once stretched four hundred miles now spans the globe; reaching points across the United States, Mexico, Canada, The Caribbean, Bermuda, Asia, The Middle-East, Europe, Africa, Australia, and numerous Trans-Pacific destinations. In 1941, the Company moved its headquarters from Monroe to Atlanta. Throughout the mega-carrier's existence, four significant mergers and acquisitions have contributed to the growth of today's Delta Air Lines. Chicago And Southern Airlines became part of Delta in 1953, providing the airline with gateways to major industry-booming destinations in the northern and southern United States. Delta's next merger with Boston-based Northeast Airlines in August 1972, gave way to routes to New England, Bermuda, Canada, and The Bahamas, along with Northeast's fleet of Douglas DC-9 and Boeing 727 aircraft, marketed as "yellowbirds", due to its infamous yellow and white paint scheme. In 1983, Delta took delivery of its first Boeing 767-200 aircraft which was cleverly named the *Spirit of Delta*, which was fully funded by voluntary contributions by the airline's employees, community partners, and retirees. The effort, named "Project 767", was lead by Delta flight attendants to promote the employees' appreciation for Delta for strong leadership and solid management during the first years following airline deregulation. The aircraft was repainted with a commemorative paint scheme to celebrate the airline's 75th anniversary in 2004, and remained as the flagship of its fleet until 2006 when it was retired and permanently parked at the Delta Heritage Museum at the Atlanta headquarters.

What could have been recognized as the most rewarding merger agreement of its time occurred in the spring of 1987, when Salt Lake City-based Western Airlines joined forces with the airline which expanded Delta's route system across the Western U.S., Mexico, Alaska, and Hawaii. As a result of the merger, Delta acquired all of Western's profitable assets including their Salt Lake City and Los Angeles hubs, and its fleet of DC-10, Boeing 737, and 727 aircraft, which were emblazoned with one of the most recognized liveries of the 1980s, their "Flying W" corporate identity. The 1991 acquisition of Pan Am's trans-Atlantic operations and the Pan Am Shuttle made Delta the largest airline between the U.S. and Europe overnight and solidified its leadership position in New York. This was the beginning of Delta's role as a global player.

It wasn't until seventeen years later when Minneapolis-based Northwest Airlines and Delta formed a merger agreement that was finalized on October 28, 2008 to form the world's largest commercial airline. From

DELTA AIR LINES

the carrier's largest hub at Hartsfield-Jackson Atlanta International Airport in Georgia, the nation's busiest airport, Delta boasts to carry more passengers on Trans-Atlantic routes than any other airline, and has done so for some time—at points dating back to the Pan Am acquisition in 1991—and only U.S. carrier to fly to every continent with the exception of Antarctica. In an attempt by Delta to compete with low-cost airlines on typical leisure-oriented routes, Delta Express began service in October, 1996, utilizing a fleet of Boeing 737-200 aircraft. The now defunct brand completely owned and operated by Delta was based at Orlando International Airport in Florida, and ceased operations in November, 2003 following the launch of Song, which launched service on April 15, 2003. Song, a single-class airline also operated by Delta operating a fleet of Boeing 757-200 aircraft, was considered a successful addition to the Northeastern U.S. to Florida market.

The fleet of bright lime green tails ceased flying on May 1, 2006, and all assets were integrated back into Delta. The Delta Connection brand—including wholly-owned subsidiaries Comair, Mesaba, and Compass Airlines; as well as separately-owned Atlantic Southeast Airlines (ASA), SkyWest, Pinnacle Airlines, Freedom Airlines, Shuttle America, and Chautauqua Airlines, continue to support the airline's domestic hubs with regional point-to-point air service. Delta's corporate identity, for most of the company's entire history, has defined by the "widget," a triangular logo that represents change and forward momentum. In 2007, Delta introduced a new livery for its fleet along with the current version of the "widget" with a brilliant new two-tone red color gradient.

Delta's Domestic Route System, 2009.

What was later on branded as SkyMiles, Delta's frequent flyer program launched in 1981 and consolidated with Northwest Airlines' WorldPerks following the merger.

Formerly known as Delta's Crown Room Club, the airline's member lounge was re-branded in 2009 as Delta Sky Club, and exists at over 56 locations throughout the airline's system. Northwest WorldClubs locations were slowly integrated into Delta's Sky Clubs which began in 2009.

28

DELTA AIR LINES

Boeing 757-200

Boeing 747-400

Facts & Figures

Founded	1928 (as Delta Air Service)
Callsign	"DELTA"
IATA designator	DL
IATA accounting	006
ICAO designator	DAL
Frequent flyer program	SkyMiles
Fleet count (including Northwest Airlines)	1,023 (+45 orders)

Delta: (5) B737-700 (+3 orders), (71) B737-800 (+34 orders), (159) B757-200, (21) B767-300 (59) B767-300ER, (21) B767-400, (8) B777-200ER, (2) B777-200LR (+5 orders), (117) MD-88 (16) MD-90. **From Northwest:** (16) B747-400, (17) B757-200ER, (16) B757-300, (57) A319-100, (69) A320-200, (11) A330-200, (21) A330-300, (71) DC-9, (78) CRJ-100, (29) CRJ-200, (15) CRJ-700 (49) CRJ-900, (49) Saab 340, (36) Embraer 175, (10) B747-200F

Total destinations	370
Total countries served	66
Parent company	Delta Air Lines, Inc.: NYSE: DAL
Headquarters	Atlanta, GA
In-flight magazine	*Sky*
Member lounge	Sky Club
Primary hub(s)	ATL, CVG, SLC, JFK, MEM, DTW, MSP, NRT
Secondary hub(s)	N/A
Subsidiaries	Comair, Mesaba, and Compass Airlines
Brands	Delta Connection, Delta Shuttle
Global Alliance	SkyTeam
Approximate number of employees	70,000
Website	delta.com
Toll-free reservations	1-800-221-1212
Route structure	Hub-and-spoke
Reservations computer system	CMS
Reservations call center locations	ATL, BKK, CVG, DFW, HIB, LON, MNL, MSP, GIG, SEA, SIN, SLC, SUX, TPA, TYO, YUL
Boeing customer code	32

2

FRONTIER

Airbus A-319, featuring *"Wally"*, Gray Wolf, N901FR

As the world's first operator of the Airbus A-318, Denver-based Frontier Airlines is the nation's largest airport's second largest air carrier, serving over 50 destinations throughout the United States, Mexico, and Costa Rica. The major low-cost airline utilizes a fleet of over 50 Airbus A-318, A-319, and A-320 aircraft along with its regional airline and main subsidiary, Lynx Aviation, which "links" smaller airport communities to the mainline carrier's central hub, and operates a fleet of 70 to 74-passenger Bombardier Q400 turboprop aircraft.

The original Frontier Airlines was Denver's hometown carrier that flew from 1946 to1986 and was among the few "local service" carriers established at the end of World War II. By the end of the 1970s, it had become the largest of the nine surviving airlines of its kind. With a vast route system linking its home at former Denver Stapleton Airport to 80 cities in 17 Western U.S. states flying white, burgundy, orange, and red Boeing 737s and McDonnell-Douglas MD-80 aircraft, carrying 87 million passengers since its inaugural flight—while maintaining an outstanding safety record.

In late 1985, Frontier found itself suffering deep financial losses after an intense competition with rivals United and Continental Airlines. The following year, the company was sold to Newark-based PEOPLExpress Airlines by its major shareholder in Akron, Ohio. As a result, PEOPLExpress, which ceased operations on February 1, 1987, terminated Frontier's operations and grounded its fleet of 42 aircraft, forcing over 4,750 personnel to unemployment. On October 17, 1986, its assets were sold to Continental Airlines – just one month before what would have been Frontier's 40th anniversary. Seven years later, in 1993, former executives and approximately 330 employees who once served for the proud airline, revitalized the name for a new airline to fly the routes that had been abandoned by Continental. The new Frontier Airlines launched its first flight on July 5, 1994 with 180 employees and two Boeing 737-200 aircraft, on routes between Denver and Bismarck, Fargo, Grand Forks, and Minot, North Dakota. Service was later added to Albuquerque, Tucson, El Paso, Billings, Bozeman, Great Falls, and Missoula, Montana from the Denver hub.

Prior to the airline's "A whole different animal" corporate slogan, the growing fleet of 737s carried "The Spirit of the West" marketing catchphrase emblazoned on the sides of the fuselage, and was expressed with eye-catching wildlife themed decals on the tails of its jets. What started out as a 21-foot high fawn, majestic mountain goat, wide-eyed raccoon, stately fox, bighorn sheep, and a grazing buffalo are now today probably the most recognizable faces in the sky, with over 50 variations; ranging from "Hector" the Sea Otter, to the ever-so-famous "Flip" the Bottlenose Dolphin—to the barbershop-style quartet Emperor Penguins: "Joe, Jim, Jay, and Gary". Frontier Airlines retired the last of its Boeing 737 aircraft on April 14, 2005 to complete their four year transition to an all-Airbus fleet.

The publically-held company emphasizes low unrestricted fares, extra leg-room, (thirty-three inches total), LiveTV on every seat-back, an all-leather interior, and an innovated frequent flyer program, EarlyReturns, which formed partnership agreements with AirTran Airways' A+ Rewards in November, 2006. Following in the footsteps of the former Frontier, the airline continues to pride itself as Denver's hometown carrier, which launched their heavily featured animated wildlife marketing campaign scheme television commercials in 2003, which helped gain

FRONTIER AIRLINES

local attention, popularity, and favoritism. The launch of these ads also helped gain a substantial 50 percent leap in brand recognition, earning top industry awards, including *New York Festivals* 'silver world medal' for the growing low-cost airline. Each animal painted on the tails of Frontier and Lynx Aviation aircraft are named, the most popular being "Larry the Lynx" and "Grizwald the Grizzly Bear". Frontier's buy-on-board meal service, "Grizwald's Gourmet Café" began on April 28, 2008, providing passengers with a variety of snack options including fresh sandwiches, fruit, nuts, and select in-flight menu items from Denver's own artisan bakery, *Udi's Handcrafted Foods*.

Frontier has been the proud recipient of the FAA Diamond Award for ten consecutive years, from 1999 through 2008. The Diamond Award recognizes carriers whose mechanics and maintenance staff complete additional training and certifications beyond that required for normal FAA certification. Frontier is the only airline to have consistently receive this award for such a period of time, as well as the only airline to ever receive this prestigious award with 100% participation from its maintenance staff, while maintaining an outstanding, flawless safety record. On August 13, 2009, Republic Airways Holdings acquired Frontier Airlines and Lynx Aviation as wholly owned subsidiaries as Frontier officially exited bankruptcy as a new airline on October 1, 2009.

The tails of the wildlife themed Airbus aircraft of Frontier Airlines.

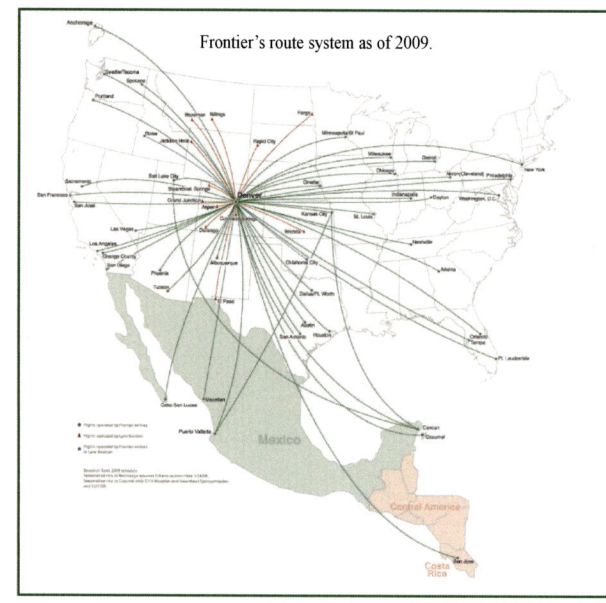

Frontier's route system as of 2009.

EarlyReturns, Frontier's frequent flyer program began on February 1, 2001 and is noted one of the fastest mileage redemption programs in the industry.

Frontier Airlines introduced "AirFairs" in 2009, a new concept which allows passengers to choose from three different levels of fares and amenities: Classic Plus, Classic, and Economy.

32

FRONTIER AIRLINES

Meet (from left to right): *"Hank the Bobcat"* (N928FR), *"Larry the Lynx"* (N929FR), and mountain lions *"Lola and Max"* (N930FR) at D.I.A.

Airbus A-320 featuring *"Colorado the Ram"*, N202FR

Facts & Figures

Founded	1993
Callsign	"FRONTIER FLIGHT"
IATA designator	F9
IATA accounting	422
ICAO designator	FFT
Frequent flyer program	EarlyReturns
Fleet count	51

(11) A318-111, (38) A319-100, (2) A320-214 (+ 8 orders), (10) Bombardier Dash 8 Q400 (Operated by Lynx Aviation).

Total destinations	58
Total countries served	3
Parent company	Republic Airways Holdings, Inc; NASDAQ: RJET
Headquarters	Denver, CO
In-flight magazine	*Wild Blue Yonder*
Member lounge	N/A
Primary hub(s)	Denver
Secondary hub(s)	N/A
Subsidiaries	Lynx Aviation
Global Alliance	N/A
Approximate number of employees	5,300
Website	frontierairlines.com
Toll-free reservations	1-800-432-1359
Route structure	Hub-and-spoke
Reservations computer system	SABRE
Reservations call center locations	Denver and Las Cruces, NM

33

Boeing 767-300ER

HAWAIIAN AIRLINES

Hawaii's largest airline, serving 20 international and domestic destinations in the Pacific Region, was incorporated on January 30, 1929 as Inter-Island Airways, LTD. It inaugurated service with scheduled passenger service between Honolulu, Maui, and the Big Island of Hawai'i. A mere total of two, eight-passenger Sikorsky S-38 amphibian planes served these three weekly round-trip flights.

Since its first scheduled flight on November 11, 1929, the carrier has provided inter-island service with high-frequency flights scheduled to five destinations on four Hawaiian Islands. In 1935, Inter-Island Airways updated its fleet as technology advanced. The airline purchased larger, 16-passenger Sikorsky S-43 aircraft to better serve its passengers and increase the capacity of its bulk airmail storage. In 1941, Inter-Island Airways changed its name to Hawaiian Airlines while introducing a newer workhorse to its fleet, the Douglas DC-3, which became a well-honored mainstay to the fleet of the islands. Hawaii's first pressurized, air conditioned cabin service was launched by the airline in 1952.

Hawaiian first ventured into long-range operations with the purchase of a Douglas DC-6A in 1958. The aircraft was converted to a DC-6C and put into service flying charters for the Military Air Transport Service between San Francisco and Japan. The company applied to the Civil Aeronautics Board for approval to fly scheduled flights between the mainland U.S. and Hawaii, but was not granted rights and ended military charter operations in 1960. Hawaiian later introduced the first all-jet service in Hawaii with the delivery of its first McDonnell Douglas DC-9 in 1966. The DC-9 reduced travel time between the islands to under 30 minutes and the fleet grew to accommodate the travel needs of a growing residential population as well as an expanding the tourism industry in the Islands.

The DC-9 remained the backbone of Hawaiian's fleet until the company replaced its entire narrow-body fleet with newer Boeing 717-200 aircraft in 2001.

DC-8 jet service entered the growing fleet in 1984 providing worldwide charter service. Scheduled service was soon launched to Pago Pago, American Samoa and Naku'alofa, Tonga. The carrier's total of three, four-engine airliners retired from the fleet in 1993. The acquisition of the airline's first wide-body jet, the Lockheed L-1011, occurred in 1985. With the launch of this aircraft, service was offered from Honolulu to the mainland with daily flights to Los Angeles. Service to San Francisco and Seattle was later added in January, 1986. Service to Western Samoa followed shortly after, expanding service in the South Pacific, including the introduction of service to Tahiti and Rarotonga in the Cook Islands in 1987. In 1994, all of Hawaiian's seven L-1011 aircraft were replaced with McDonnell-Douglas DC-10s, leased from American Airlines, eventually operating 10 DC-10-10s and four DC-10-30 aircraft until it replaced its entire wide-body fleet with 14 Boeing 767-300ER aircraft in 2001 and 2002.

The airline holds an unbroken safety record after 80 years in operation while maintaining one of the youngest fleets in the industry. As a pioneer of Pacific aviation, Hawaiian Airlines currently upholds a growing domestic and international network, transporting tourists and businesspeople between the mainland and Hawaii and the South Pacific with a fleet of Boeing 717 and 767 aircraft. Destinations within the Lower 48 states across the Western U.S. Region include six cities in California, Phoenix, Las Vegas, Portland, and Seattle/Tacoma. International services to routes in the South Pacific include Pago Pago, American Samoa;

Papeete, Tahiti; Sydney, Australia; and Manila, Philippines. In 2010, the airline will take delivery of its first A330-200 aircraft, launching its next long-range widebody fleet renewal and expansion which will eventually replace any existing 767 aircraft with an all-new Airbus fleet. In addition to up to 15 new A330s, the future fleet plan calls for Hawaiian to be among the first U.S. carriers to take delivery of the latest-technology, the Airbus A350-800XWB, with six on firm order for deliveries starting in 2017 and purchase rights for six additional aircraft of this type.

Hawaiian's livery consists of brightly colored jets reflecting the warm tones of its island origin, and carrying a profile of an island girl named "Pualani," meaning "flower of the sky." Unveiled in 1975, the symbol has since been modernized and serves as the airline's proud and vibrant logo. The carrier maintains its hub, main facilities, headquarters, and main operations center at Honolulu International Airport and operates a secondary hub at Maui's Kahului Airport.

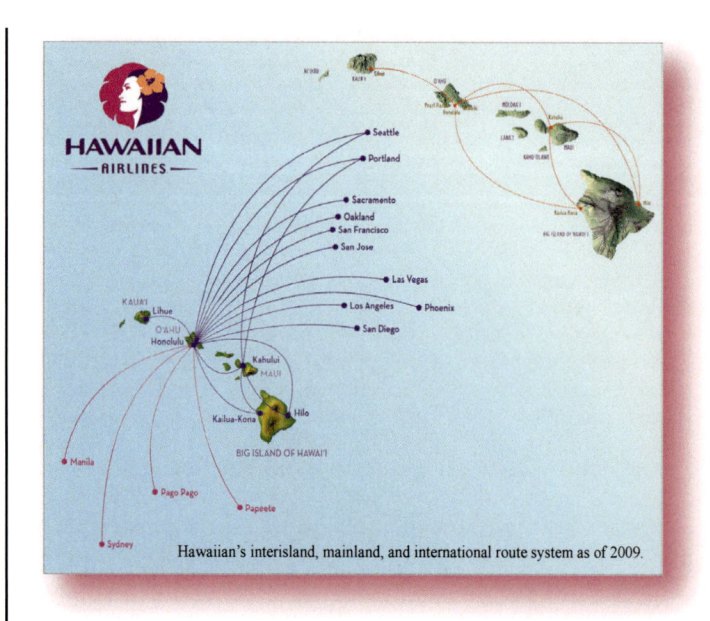

Hana Hou!, the inflight magaaine of Hawaiian Airlines.

Hawaiian's interisland, mainland, and international route system as of 2009.

Hawaiian Airlines' frequent flyer program, HawaiianMiles, include top-tier levels designated as Pualani Gold and Pualani Platinum. Partnerships include various domestic U.S. and international airlines.

Premier Club, Hawaiian's member lounge, has locations in Hilo, Honolulu, Kahului, Kona, Lihue, and Los Angeles.

HAWAIIAN AIRLINES

Boeing 717-200

Boeing 767-300ER

Facts & Figures

Founded	1929 (as Inter-Island Airways LTD.)
Callsign	"HAWAIIAN"
IATA designator	HA
IATA accounting	173
ICAO designator	HAL
Frequent flyer program	HawaiianMiles
Fleet count	33

(14) 767-300ER, (4) 767-300, (15) 717-200, (0) A330-200 (9 orders, 6 options), (0) A350-800XWB (6 orders, 6 options for 2017-2020)

Total destinations	20
Total countries served	4
Parent company	Hawaiian Holdings, Inc.; NASDAQ: HA
Headquarters	Honolulu, HI
In-flight magazine	*Hana Hou!*
Member lounge	Premier Club
Primary hub(s)	Honolulu, HI
Secondary hub(s)	N/A
Subsidiaries	N/A
Global Alliance	N/A
Approximate number of employees	3,700
Website	hawaiianairlines.com
Toll-free reservations	1-800-367-5320
Route structure	Hub-and-spoke
Reservations computer system	SABRE
Reservations call center locations	Baguio, Philippines
Boeing Customer Code	2A

37

jetBlue AIRWAYS

Airbus A320-200: *"I (heart) Blue"*

38

JETBLUE AIRWAYS

JetBlue Airways, the largest operator of the Airbus A320 and launch customer of the Embraer 190, began service on February 11, 2000 with an inaugural flight between New York and Fort Lauderdale. The now famed carrier whose paint livery is one of the most easily recognized, currently functions as one of the nation's leading low-cost airlines and is based out at New York's JFK International Airport.

JetBlue's origins date back to 1993 when CEO David Neeleman, a former Southwest Airlines employee, sold his first airline—Salt Lake City-based Morris Air, to Southwest Airlines. As a founder and President of the former carrier, Neeleman proved that innovative, high-quality airline service coupled with low fares will attract a strong and loyal market. Following the sale of Morris Air, Neeleman went on to help launch WestJet, a successful Canadian low-fare carrier, and to further develop the e-ticketing system he had implemented at Morris Air into Open Skies, an airline reservation system, in which he sold to Hewlett Packard in 1999.

With three victorious aviation businesses on his resume, Neeleman decided the time was right to bring his airline formula to the world's largest aviation market, New York City. In July 1999, having secured a select team of management and $130 million in capital funding from investors such as Weston Presidio Capital, George Soros and Chase Capital, Neeleman surprised the aviation industry with the announcement of his plan to launch a new airline. He founded the Company in February 1999 under the name "NewAir". Following the decision to rename his new airline "JetBlue", the airline began its primitive stages by following Southwest's approach of offering low-cost travel, but sought to distinguish itself with amenities such as in-flight entertainment, seats equipped with televisions, and satellite radio. In his own words, Neeleman's vision was "to bring humanity back to air travel." In September 1999, just three months before taking delivery of its first Airbus A320 aircraft, the airline was awarded an unprecedented exemption for 75 initial take off and landing slots at John F. Kennedy International Airport, and received formal U.S. authorization in February 2000, when it officially launched operations.

By December 2002, just two years after opening its doors, the airline had nearly flown its ten millionth customer and serviced 20 cities within the United States and Puerto Rico. As of 2009, JetBlue operates 600 flights a day to 60 cities, including all three NYC airports. The company has since become the largest airline serving JFK and specializes in non-stop flights to and from New York and the West Coast, Florida, and the Caribbean. Each of JetBlue's aircraft bears a unique name—and in some way incorporates the name of the color 'blue' in the title. Names such as "Blue Suede Shoes", "Brand Spankin' Blue" and "Blue 100" to commemorate the delivery of the airline's 100th Airbus A320 on March 23, 2007, were all names given to individual aircraft by the airline's employees.

The carrier attests to the notion that low-cost shouldn't mean lack of service. JetBlue's Airbus A320 and Embraer 190 aircraft are among the youngest in the industry, with all leather seating, and free DIRECTV satellite programming on each seat-back which includes 36 channels. DIRECTV is not available on flights outside of the continental U.S, but movies on these routes are offered free of charge. XM Satellite Radio is also another added service for its customers. All of JetBlue's aircraft aircraft have a single-class configuration—the A320 with 150 seats, and Embraer 190 which seats 100. In 2007, Lufthansa German Airlines

JETBLUE AIRWAYS

purchased a 19 percent ownership interest in JetBlue. In February of the same year, JetBlue unveiled a "Customer Bill of Rights", a first in the airline industry, which pledges it will notify customers in advance in the event of delays, cancellations and diversions, and outlines denied boarding compensation and other reimbursement promises.

Having accomplished several milestones, JetBlue Airways also boasts numerous awards and accolades since its initiation into service. Among the many, the airline was rated the number one U.S. domestic airline by Conde Nast Traveler magazine's "Readers' Choice Awards" for the sixth year in a row, in October 2007. On June 17, 2008, it ranked 'Highest in Customer Satisfaction Among Low Cost Carriers in North America' by J.D. Power and Associates, a customer satisfaction recognition received for the fourth year in a row. The carrier was ranked "Best North American Low Cost Airline" with a four-star salute by Skytrax, the official world airline and airport star rating program, based in the United Kingdom.

In October, 2008, JetBlue opened the doors to its brand new spacious, state-of-the-art Terminal Five ("T5") at its hub at JFK International Airport in New York, which has received astonishing reviews from the media, the public and throughout the industry.

Various tail designs of JetBlue aircraft.

JetBlue's destinations as of 2009.

JetBlue launched TrueBlue, a 'customer appreciation program' on June 18, 2002.

JetBlue Airways' "Customer Bill of Rights" is recognized as an 'industry first', which promotes the welfare of its customers.

JETBLUE AIRWAYS

Airbus A320, N521JB: *"Baby Blue"*

Embraer 190: *"Dream Come Blue"*

Facts & Figures

Founded	2000
Callsign	"JETBLUE"
IATA designator	B6
IATA accounting	279
ICAO designator	JBU
Frequent flyer program	TrueBlue
Fleet count	144

(110) Airbus A320-200 (w/ 57 orders), (34) Embraer 190 (w/64 orders)

Total destinations	60
Total countries served	10
Parent company	JetBlue Airways Corp.: NASDAQ: JBLU
Headquarters	Forest Hills, NY
In-flight magazine	N/A
Member lounge	N/A
Primary hub(s)	New York/Kennedy
Focus Cities	JFK, BOS, FLL, LGB, MCO, IAD.
Subsidiaries	N/A
Global Alliance	N/A
Approximate number of employees	11,800
Website	jetblue.com
Toll-free reservations	1-800-538-2583
Route structure	Point-to-point
Reservations computer system	Navitaire; SABRE (2010)
Reservations call center locations	Salt Lake City (virtual)

41

MIDWEST AIRLINES

Boeing 717-200

MIDWEST AIRLINES

Formerly Midwest Express Airlines, Milwaukee-based Midwest Airlines grew out of Kimberly-Clark Corporation's internal transportation service to transport sales executives and engineers to remote mill locations beginning in 1948. Kimberly-Clark formed K-C Aviation in 1969 as a subsidiary providing aviation services and specializing in the meticulous customization of corporate aircraft; it began operation of a DC-9 corporate shuttle in 1982. The popularity of the shuttle, and continued frustration on the part of Kimberly-Clark executives with the inadequacies of commercial service, evolved into the launch of Midwest Express as a scheduled passenger airline on June 11, 1984.

Midwest Express began with 83 employees and a fleet of two DC-9-15 aircraft flying daily nonstops from Milwaukee's General Mitchell International Airport to Appleton, Boston, and Dallas/Ft. Worth. Over the years, Midwest added additional DC-9s and introduced McDonnell Douglas MD-81, 82, and 88 aircraft to the fleet, while expanding service to major business and leisure destinations coast to coast. Their longtime corporate slogan, "The best care in the air," emerged from certain features and services the airline offered. As part of their "Signature Service," the most well known are their chocolate chip cookies, baked right on board and served warm. Passengers enjoyed this popular treat following sumptuous meals ranging from fine seafood and fresh fruit to delectable deserts, served on china with complimentary wine or champagne while relaxing in luxurious, wide leather seats only two-across – all offered at a "coach fare or less" pricing structure.

Following financial difficulties that many airlines experienced following the September 11, 2001 tragedies, Midwest discontinued its complimentary meal service and replaced it with a buy-onboard product, Best Care Cuisine – which offers chef-prepared, made-from-scratch meals. In 2003, Midwest Express renamed itself Midwest Airlines, due to the association of the word "Express" with small regional airlines. At the same time, Midwest's commuter subsidiary Skyway Airlines, The Midwest Express Connection, became Midwest Connect. By 2008, Midwest's fleet of DC-9 and MD-80 series aircraft were replaced with more modern, fuel-efficient, cost-effective Boeing 717 aircraft. Today Midwest Airlines offers its unique "Midwest Class" service, featuring its wide leather Signature seating as part of one-cabin service that also offers all-leather two-by-three "Saver" seating.

In early 2008, the airline's publicly traded parent company, Midwest Air Group, was acquired by the private Texas investment firm, TPG Capital. Later that year, Skyway ceased air service and transitioned to a ground handling company for Midwest and other carriers. Under an air services agreement, Indianapolis-based Republic Airways, operated by Republic Airlines, operates 76-passenger Embraer E-170 aircraft, and operated by Chautauqua Airlines, a Republic Airways Company, are 50-passenger Embraer 145 and 37-passenger Embraer 135 aircraft, – all of which are painted in the Midwest Connect livery.

Midwest's commitment to offering personal, attentive service has earned it national and international recognition from frequent travelers and the industry, including *Condé Nast Traveler*, *Travel+Leisure* and the *Zagat Airline Survey* – which have rated Midwest the best airline in the U.S. – and the *Freddie Awards*, which have recognized the Midwest Miles frequent flyer program for best customer service. The airline that calls Milwaukee home is also the recipient of the Federal Aviation Administration's Diamond Maintenance Award, presented in 2006.

43

MIDWEST AIRLINES

Midwest Airlines' Route System, 2009

Midwest Class features 40 of the airline's extra-wide leather "Signature Seats" in a two-by-two configuration with 35-36 inches of legroom, along with 59 newly designed leather "Saver Seats" in a three-by-two configuration with 32 inches of legroom. The new seating design provides the greatest percentage of enhanced-comfort coach seating of any domestic airline. Passengers in both types of seats receive the same exceptional service for which the airline is known.

■ ■ ■ ■

Midwest Airlines' 'little touch' that made a huge difference has been served warm on Midwest flights since 1986. The chocolate chip cookie, made with the airline's own recipe, remains a mainstay throughout the airline, and is also available for purchase at grocery stores and professional sporting events in Milwaukee and Kansas City.

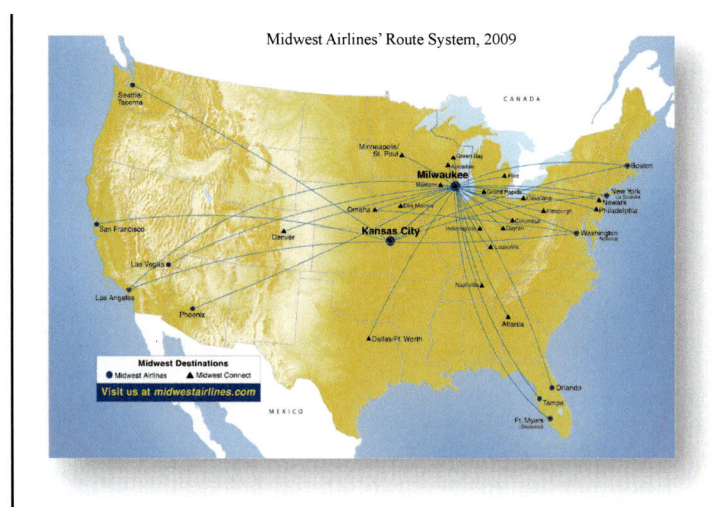

One of the most rewarding frequent flyer programs in the industry, the Midwest Miles program offers a variety of ways to earn and redeem miles on Midwest Airlines and Midwest Connect. In 2009, *Inside Flyer* magazine's Freddie Awards awarded Midwest #1 Best Customer Service – for the fourth consecutive year.

MIDWEST MILES

Members of Midwest Airlines' *Best Care Club* enjoy exclusive benefits. The airline's airport club is located at Milwaukee's General Mitchell International Airport in the "D" Concourse near Gate 38.

BEST CARE CLUB
MIDWEST AIRLINES

MIDWEST AIRLINES

Boeing 717-200

Boeing 717-200

Facts & Figures

Founded	1984 (as Midwest Express)
Callsign	"MIDEX"
IATA designator	YX
IATA accounting	453
ICAO designator	MEP
Frequent flyer program	Midwest Miles
Fleet count	33

(9) B717-200, and operated by Republic Airlines as Midwest Connect: (7) Embraer E-135, (5) Embraer E-145, and (12) Embraer E-170

Total destinations	33
Total countries served	1
Parent company	Republic Airways Holdings, Inc.; NASDAQ: RJET
Headquarters	Oak Creek, WI
In-flight magazine	*My Midwest*
Member lounge	Best Care Club
Primary hub(s)	Milwaukee, WI
Secondary hub(s)	Kansas City
Subsidiaries	Skyway Airlines (ground handling)
Brands	Midwest Connect
Global Alliance	N/A
Approximate number of employees	1,640
Website	midwestairlines.com
Toll-free reservations	1-800-452-2022
Route structure	Hub-and-spoke
Reservations computer system	SABRE
Reservations call center locations	Milwaukee
Boeing customer code	BL

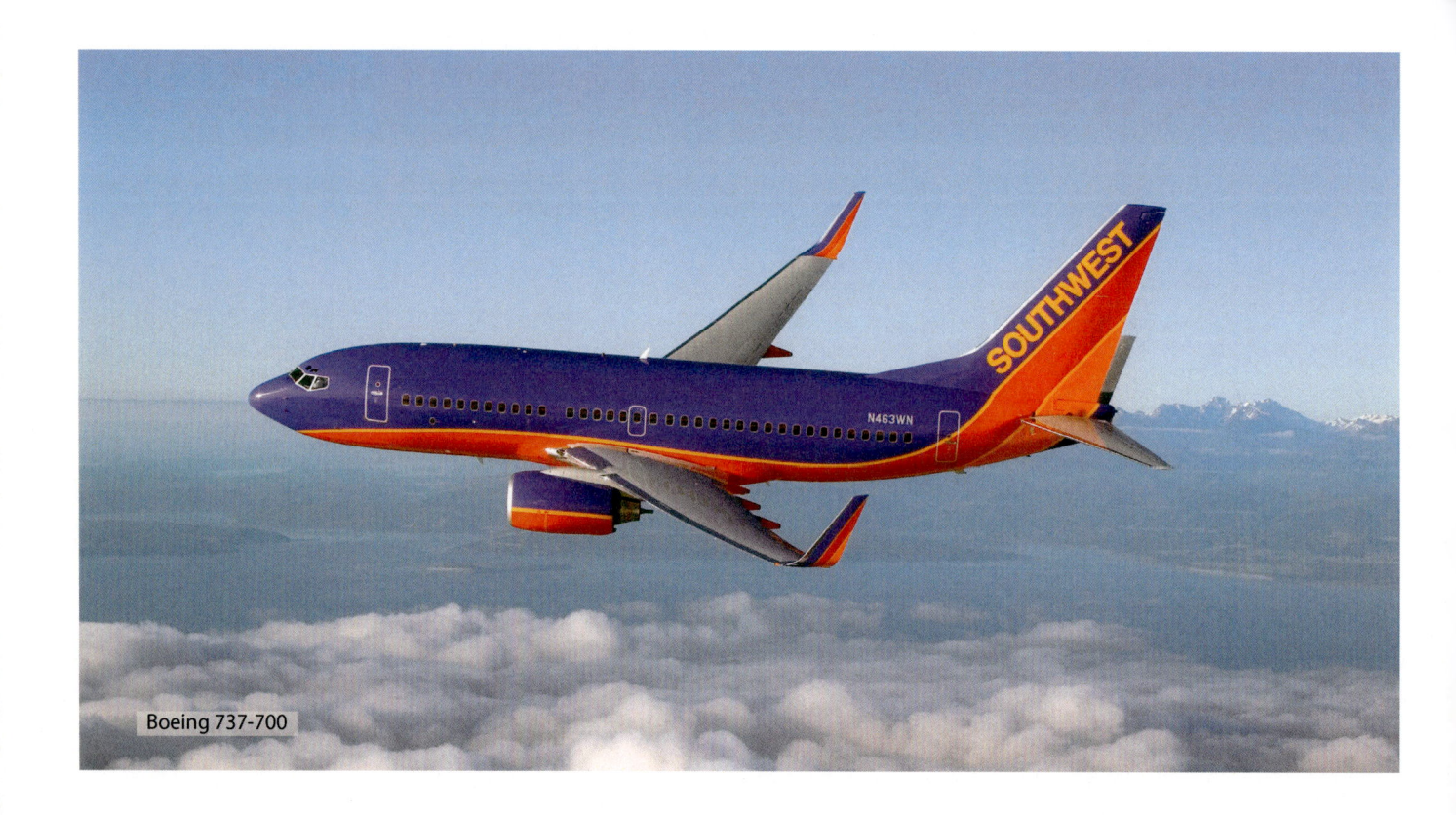

SOUTHWEST

Boeing 737-700

SOUTHWEST AIRLINES

The "Airline that 'LUV' Built" was incorporated on March 15, 1967 as Air Southwest, and soon after renamed Southwest Airlines, based in Dallas Love Field, Texas. This once small intra-Texas carrier launched service on June 18, 1971 and has since become one of the largest and most popular low-fare airlines in America. It utilizes an all-jet fleet consisting entirely of Boeing 737 aircraft, and had touted itself as "THE COMPANY PLANE" for its convenient schedules, high frequency service, and competitive fares.

This unique and "fun loving" carrier has had a colorful and an exciting history. In the early years, Southwest faced tense competition from the much larger former Braniff International Airlines. However, the carrier's unflappable founding fathers, including Lamar Muse, William Franklin, and cofounders Rollin King and Herbert D. Kelleher, who was appointed Company President on March 28, 1978; ventured several successful public relations and marketing ploys. Despite all odds, stiff competition, and legal challenges, Southwest Airlines, "the airline that love built" still flourishes. The small Texas airline initiated service to only three Texas cities – Dallas, Houston, and San Antonio, with six daily round-trip flights from Dallas to San Antonio and twelve round trips from Dallas to Houston Intercontinental.

After several mergers and acquisitions, including Muse Air, another Texas-based carrier formed by Lamar Muse, on June 25, 1983; and Morris Air, a Salt Lake City-based carrier on December 31, 1993; Southwest continued to profit from retaining a similar operational approach and overall structure similar to its predecessors. When King and Kelleher got together and decided to start a different kind of airline, they began with one simplistic notion: "If you get your passengers to their destinations when they want to get there, on time, at the lowest possible fares, and make darn sure they have a good time doing it, people will fly your airline." Based on the airline's successful "freedom fighting" past and bright future, the airline that employs well over 35,000 employees hold that statement as a time-honored proclamation.

Flying one of the youngest fleets in the nation, with an average age of approximately nine years, are specialty aircraft—including three flying killer whales, the *"Shamu"* aircraft, *"Lone Star One"*, painted in the colors of the State of Texas' flag; *"Arizona One"*, a symbol of the importance of the state of Arizona to Southwest Airlines; *"California One"*, featuring a livery with the State flag; *"Silver One"*, its 25th Anniversary plane; *"Triple Crown One"*, dedicated to the Employees of Southwest Airlines for their achievements of five consecutive annual Triple Crown awards; *"Nevada One"*, a high-flying tribute to the state of Nevada; *"New Mexico One"*, also known as *Zia*—painted in the bright yellow of the New Mexico state flag; *"Maryland One"*, emblazoned with an artist's rendering of the Maryland state flag; *"Slam Dunk One"*, symbolizing Southwest's special partnership with the National Basketball Association; and the newest addition that debuted in the spring of 2008—*"Illinois One"*, featuring the flag of the Prairie State.

Today, Southwest's fleet of over 500 deep canyon blue airplanes (in which all 737-300 and 500 series were retrofitted with an all-leather interior and 700 series delivered as such), replaced the Company's traditional desert gold, warm red, and bright orange colors which served well for over 30 years, service 67 cities across the country, with more than 3,200 flights per day. Pioneers of large scale point-to-point service, Southwest maintains the largest passenger fleet of Boeing 737 aircraft of

47

all airlines based in the United States. Las Vegas' McCarran International Airport is the carrier's largest focus city, followed by Chicago/Midway, Phoenix, Baltimore-Washington, Houston/Hobby, Dallas Love Field, Oakland, Los Angeles, Orlando, Pittsburgh, Philadelphia, San Diego, Tampa, Nashville, Austin, and Denver.

Since 1987, when the Department of Transportation began tracking Customer Satisfaction statistics, Southwest has consistently led the entire airline industry with the lowest ratio of complaints per passengers boarded. Many airlines have looked to Southwest as an appropriate business model, and the Culture of Southwest is admired and emulated by numerous corporations and organizations. Always the innovator, Southwest pioneered Senior Fares, a same-day air freight delivery service, and Ticketless Travel. Southwest led the way with the first airline web page—southwest.com, the first-ever direct link to Customer's computer desktops that delivers live updates on the hottest deals, and the first airline corporate blog, *Nuts About Southwest*. Their 'Share the Spirit' community programs make Southwest the hometown airline of every city they serve. The Company is proud in boasting their accomplishments, and along the way they've earned a title no other airline in the industry can claim: The only short and medium to long-haul, low-fare, high-frequency, point-to-point, legacy carrier in America.

Southwest's destinations as of 2009.

"Maryland One", a Boeing 737-800 (N214WN), joined Southwest's fleet in 2005, comemmorating the airline's dedicated service in the Baltimore/Washington area and recognizing it as "A high flying tribute to The State of Maryland".

Pioneering web-based reservations, the Company's website debuted in 1996, introducing "Ticketless Travel" to the growing online community.

Southwest's unveiled it's famed frequent flyer program, "Rapid Rewards" in 1996, as the airline celebrated 25 years of service.

48

SOUTHWEST AIRLINES

Boeing 737-700 blended winglet

A Boeing 737-700 departing McCarran International Airport serving Las Vegas, Nevada

Facts & Figures

Founded	1967 (as Air Southwest)
Callsign	"SOUTHWEST"
IATA designator	WN
IATA accounting	526
ICAO designator	SWA
Frequent flyer program	Rapid Rewards
Fleet count	542
	(185) B737-300, (25) B737-500, (332) B737-700 w/ (101) orders, (62) options, (54) rights
Total destinations	67
Total countries served	1
Parent company	Southwest Airlines, Co.; NYSE: LUV
Headquarters	Dallas, TX
In-flight magazine	*Spirit* magazine
Member lounge	N/A
Primary hub(s)	Dallas Love Field
Focus cities	LAS, MDW, PHX, BWI, HOU, DAL, OAK, LAX, MCO, DEN
Subsidiaries	N/A
Global Alliance	N/A
Approximate number of employees	35,000
Website	southwest.com
Toll-free reservations	1-800-435-9792
Route structure	point-to-point
Reservations computer system	SABRE
Reservations call center locations	Chicago, Oklahoma City, Phoenix, Albuquerque, Houston, and San Antonio.
Boeing customer code	H4

spirit airlines

Airbus A319

SPIRIT AIRLINES

Spirit Airlines, pioneers of "Ultra Low Fares" in the Americas, was founded in 1980 in Eastpointe, Michigan. The company began as Charter One, a Detroit-based charter tour operator providing travel packages to entertainment destinations such as Atlantic City, Las Vegas, and the Bahamas. Ten years later, Charter One began scheduled service from Boston and Providence, Rhode Island to Atlantic City, New Jersey. On May 29, 1992, Charter One brought jet equipment into the fleet, changed its name to Spirit Airlines, and inaugurated service from Detroit to Atlantic City.

In April 1993, Spirit Airlines began scheduled service to destinations in Florida. During the next five years the airline expanded rapidly, increasing service from Detroit and adding service in new markets such as Myrtle Beach, South Carolina; Los Angeles and New York. Spirit relocated its headquarters in December 1999, moving from Eastpointe, Michigan to Miramar, Florida. Expansion continued with the addition of the Chicago market, as well as coast-to-coast service to Los Angeles. In November 2001, Spirit inaugurated service to San Juan, Puerto Rico, and implemented a fully-integrated Spanish language customer service plan, including a website and dedicated reservations and information line. May and June 2002 brought new service to Las Vegas, Nevada, as well as expanded service in nearly every market of the airline's route system. In the fall of 2003, the airline launched service to Washington, D.C.'s Reagan National Airport and Cancun, Mexico.

In fall 2004, Spirit introduced service to Santo Domingo, the capital of the Dominican Republic; and premier vacation destination in the Caribbean Sea. Spirit began its transition to an all-Airbus fleet in fall 2004 which was completed in September 2006, thus becoming an all-Airbus airline. The airline touts itself as having the youngest fleet of Airbus aircraft in the Americas, consisting of Airbus A319s, seating 145 passengers, and A321s, seating 218. The carrier's new fleet was designed with customers in mind with all leather seats, moveable headrests, and extra large overhead bins.

The airline's goal of becoming the leading low cost carrier to the Caribbean became a reality in mid 2005 to late 2006, with new flights to the Bahamas, Jamaica, and U.S. Virgin Islands. Additional service to the Caribbean began in 2007 to Haiti, Aruba, and St. Maarten/St. Martin, as well as increased service to Puerto Rico via Aguadilla and Ponce. Low cost service to Latin America began in 2007 with service to Costa Rica, Guatemala, Honduras, and Nicaragua in Central America, and new service to Peru in South America. In 2007, the airline unveiled its new "ultra low cost carrier" brand that celebrates the colors of the Caribbean and Latin America regions. The company's energetic new colors were unveiled to reinforce Spirit's four brand principles include: *caliente red* for low fares, *environmental green* for on-time performance and reliability, *sunshine yellow* for clean new planes, and *ocean blue* for its friendly staff. In 2008, Spirit continued to add more flights, including new service to Boston, as well as more flights to the Caribbean and Latin America with new service to Panama City, Panama; and Cartagena and Bogota, Colombia. In 2009, Spirit began new service to Santiago, Dominican Republic and Medellin, Colombia, with added service to Armenia, Colombia which was scheduled to start by the end of the year.

Today, Spirit Airlines' ULCC (Ultra Low Cost Carrier) approach "liberates customers from being forced into paying for services they do not want or use. When customers are seeking the best value in travel, they

SPIRIT AIRLINES

choose a low fare at spiritair.com and select the services and options appropriate for their travel needs. Spirit's ultra low cost model, driven from numerous efficiencies, new aircraft, advanced technology and dedicated staff, allows the airline to take this approach, offering savings to millions of customers in the United States, Caribbean, Central and South America."

Spirit Airlines, the largest ULCC in the United States, Latin America and the Caribbean, has more than 150 daily flights to 39 destinations in the Americas.

Skylights, The in-flight magazine of Spirit Airlines

Spirit Airlines' route system as of 2009.

Members of Spirit Airlines' $9 Fare Club gain private access to ultra low fare member-only sales with fares often starting in the single digits – sometimes even as low as a penny.

FREE SPIRIT™ is Spirit's frequent flyer program that offers award travel on every flight without black-out dates.

SPIRIT AIRLINES

Airbus A-319

Airbus A-319

Facts & Figures

Founded	1980 (as Charter One)
Callsign	"SPIRIT WINGS"
IATA designator	NK
IATA accounting	487
ICAO designator	NKS
Frequent flyer program	FREE SPIRIT
Fleet count	28

(26) Airbus A319-100, (2) Airbus A321-200

Total destinations	40
Total countries served	17
Parent company	Spirit Airlines, Inc. (private ownership)
Headquarters	Miramar, FL
In-flight magazine	*Skylights*
Member lounge	N/A
Primary hub(s)	Fort Lauderdale-Hollywood
Secondary hub(s)	N/A
Subsidiaries	N/A
Global Alliance	N/A
Approximate number of employees	2,300
Website	spiritair.com
Toll-free reservations	1-800-772-7117
Route structure	Hub-and-spoke
Reservations computer system	SkySpeed
Reservations call center locations	India and Costa Rica

53

sun country airlines

Boeing 737-800, bearing a logo commemmorating the airline's 25 years of service.

54

SUN COUNTRY AIRLINES

Headquartered in one of the Twin Cities' premier suburbs of Mendota Heights, Minnesota, Sun Country Airlines traces its roots to 1982 where a group of pilots and flight attendants from the defunct Braniff International Airlines joined together to form their own airline with the help of businessmen in the Twin Cities of Minneapolis and Saint Paul, Minnesota. This group named their venture Sun Country Airlines and partnered with locally based MLT Vacations and exclusively operated charter flights. Sun Country's inaugural flight was on board a former Braniff Boeing 727-200 which on January 30, 1983 flew from Sioux Falls, South Dakota to Las Vegas, Nevada.

The start-up airline had 33 employees which included the Company's first president, Captain Jim Olsen, who was also Chief Pilot, and his wife, Joan Smith-Olsen, who acted as Head of Inflight Operations and Chief Flight Attendant. The employees assumed many positions at the airline and their duties included tasks that went beyond their job description. Flight attendants stocked liquor kits and beverages along with preparing meals, while pilots updated flight manuals and assisted in catering. The entire group assisted in cleaning the aircraft exterior to the interior while managing to maintain a 98% on-time performance record in their first year.

Slow and deliberate expansion through the 1980s created steady profits for the Company. In 1986, the company entered the McDonnell-Douglas DC-10, leased from Northwest Airlines, into service which enabled the airline to serve charter flights to new international routes from its Minneapolis hub to Oslo, Norway and military charters to Saudi Arabia and Bahrain. In 1989, Sun Country became a member of the Civil Reserve Air Fleet (CRAF) where many military charter flights were flown to serve Desert Storm efforts in 1990-1991. For their efforts in supporting the operation, 130 of the Company's employees were recognized by the United States Air Force. The airline received record earnings of $9.7 million in 1991, and doubled its fleet and workforce. That same year, the airline acquired additional Boeing 727 and DC-10 aircraft to upkeep the demands from several tour operators that had chosen the profitable, successful charter air carrier.

On June 1, 1999 the airline prided itself in becoming a scheduled air carrier. Although passenger loads were favorable, the increased expenses that coincided with their new status deemed difficult and unmanageable to cover. Price wars hurt the airline as a result, and by 2000 Sun Country had suffered a tremendous loss of $62 million. The terrorist attacks of September 11, 2001 were yet another blow for the airline. On December 8, 2001, Sun Country Airlines announced it was ceasing scheduled operations and shut its doors completely just a few days later. Shortly thereafter, a group of investors purchased Sun Country and resumed flight operations in early 2002. As Sun Country grew, additional capital was needed for expansion. Two Twin Cities firms, Petters Aviation and Whitebox Advisors, joined together to acquire the airline in 2006 and began implementing a conservative growth plan. In November, 2007, Petters Aviation, LLC purchased all of the equity interest of Whitebox Advisors.

The Company filed for Chapter 11 bankruptcy protection on October 6, 2008 and has since continued normal operations; but the current stock ownership of the Company has been transferred to the control of a court-appointed receiver, Doug Kelley. Fortunately, it announced a profit for the first quarter of 2009 - operating income was $9.8 million and operat-

SUN COUNTRY AIRLINES

Sun Country Airlines operates a fleet of Boeing 737-700 and 800 series aircraft for both domestic and charter flights throughout the United States, Mexico, and the Caribbean from its hub at Minneapolis/St. Paul International Airport's Humphrey Terminal. Sun Country was ranked in the Top Ten Domestic Airlines by both Travel+Leisure and *Condé Nast Traveler* magazines for three consecutive years and continues to serve as "Minnesota's Hometown Airline".

Sun Country's route system as of 2009.

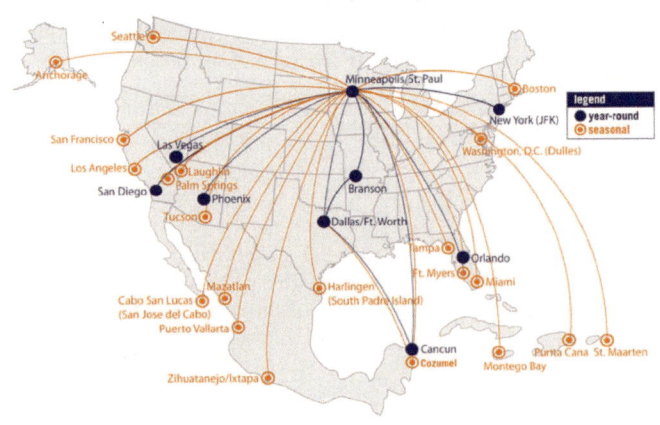

U*fly* Rewards, the airline's frequent flyer program, was launched in July, 2007 and is based on a point system versus the typical air mileage accrual program most traditional programs offer.

Formerly named VIP Club, Sun Country's U*fly* Rewards Plus program is unique in the sense that it does not operate on a mileage nor point-based scale, but rather offers paid members the right to unprecedented low fares and are available up to one day in advance of travel.

56

SUN COUNTRY AIRLINES

Boeing 737-800s at MSP

Boeing 737 tail fins

Facts & Figures

Founded	1982
Callsign	"SUN COUNTRY"
IATA designator	SY
IATA accounting	337
ICAO designator	SCX
Frequent flyer program	U*Fly* Rewards
Fleet count	12
	(10) B737-800 (first class and coach), (2) B737-700 (coach only)
Total destinations	28
Total countries served	5
Parent company	MN Airlines, LLC (privately owned)
Headquarters	Mendota Heights, MN
In-flight magazine	*Sun Country* (formerly *Escape* Magazine)
Member lounge	N/A
Primary hub(s)	Minneapolis/St. Paul
Secondary hub(s)	N/A
Subsidiaries	N/A
Global Alliance	N/A
Approximate number of employees	1,200
Website	suncountry.com
Toll-free reservations	1-800-359-6786
Route structure	Hub-and-spoke
Reservations computer system	SABRE
Reservations call center locations	Mendota Heights, MN
Boeing Customer Code	N/A

57

UNITED

Boeing 777-200

Photo courtesy of Alan Pingstone

United Airlines is the world's third largest airline by revenue passenger miles, and operates more than 3,000 flights per day, including 540 daily scheduled departures from its largest hub at Chicago's O'Hare International Airport in Illinois. San Francisco International Airport in California is home to United's third-largest hub, and Maintenance Operations Center, the airline's largest maintenance hub.

The history of the oldest existing commercial airline in the United States begins with a flight operated by Varney Air Lines, a mail service carrier, and piloted by Leon "Lee" Cuddeback on April 6, 1926. On that day, the open-cockpit swallow biplane flew from Pasco, Washington to Elko, Nevada via Boise, Idaho. As a result, United Air Lines was organized as a management company for Varney, Boeing Air Transport, National Air Transport, and Pacific Air Transport on July 1, 1931. Service from San Francisco to Chicago emerged the introduction of flight attendant services in 1930. Ellen Church was the world's first flight attendant, flying on board a twelve-passenger Boeing 80-A, along with seven other stewardesses. Other airlines soon followed United's lead.

The first flight kitchen, belonging to United, was established in Oakland, California in December of 1936, where in-flight meals were prepared. In that same year, United introduced the 21-passnger DC-3, which revolutionized the world of air transportation. By 1937, the airline introduced "Skylounge" service between New York and Chicago. Overnight sleeper-service was later initiated on flights coast-to-coast. The first jet aircraft entered United's fleet in June, 1959. It was the "Overwater Super" Douglas DC-8 of which 30 orders were placed for $175 million. The DC-8s flew nonstop from Honolulu to Chicago on a 7 hour and 52 minute journey. On June 1, 1961, United and Capital Airlines merged to create the world's largest airline. In 1974, the airline commissioned Los Angeles designer Saul Bass to develop a contemporary new logo. It featured a stylized red and blue "U" symbol and nicknamed the "tulip". The logo remains in use today with slight modification only when displayed on the tail section. Guidelines were established to ensure the consistent appearance of the logo in all applications. Soon after, the airline giant moved its hub from Midway Airport in Chicago to a 51-acre office complex near Chicago's O'Hare International Airport. Mileage Plus, the airline's frequent traveler program, was introduced on May 6, 1981.

On July 25, 1994, a historic move was made by United's stockholders. For the first time in the airline's history, representatives from the International Association of Machinists and the Air Line Pilots Association were added to the board of directors. Salaried and management employees also selected an outside director to sit on the board. Over the next two years, the original 54,000 U.S. employees who launched the Employee Stock Ownership Plan (ESOP) in mid-1994 were joined in ownership by many of their co-workers in Europe, South America, and Asia. As it flew toward the new millennium, United continued to lead commercial aviation. With the establishment of its ESOP in July 1994, United became the largest employee majority-owned corporation in the world.

The Star Alliance global partnership the carrier formed in 1997 with four international carriers continued to grow and expand United's reach. For the first time since 1965, the company departed from its familiar "friendly skies" advertising slogan, replacing it with the term "'Rising." The slogan that was adopted in 2004, "It's Time to Fly", remains today as their current marketing and advertising campaign. In 2009, United gradually phased operations of their own low-cost airline marketing brand, TED, which primarily flew Airbus A-320 aircraft to popular tourist destinations within the United States and Mexico from all of the carrier's hubs.

The name, TED, was derived from the last three letters of the name United and lasted six years. This venture was formed to compete with other low-cost carriers such as Southwest and especially Frontier Airlines, who also shares their main hubs in Denver, including a new wave of low-cost carriers, and was discontinued due to failed attempts to target these low-cost markets. This is the second marketing brand the airline created, following *Shuttle by United* service, flying fleet of all-737 aircraft operated flights on the U.S. West Coast, established as an "airline within an airline", which ceased operations in 2001 and lasted for seven years. At the same time, Delta Air Lines' similar operation of now defunct Song failed for similar reasons. United continues to maintain a vision of global expansion, after successfully emerging from a four year bankruptcy that ended in 2006, recorded as the longest in airline history. The airline continues to focus on its international presence, particularly in the People's Republic of China, to cities such as Shanghai, Beijing, and Hong Kong, from most of its major hubs in Chicago, San Francisco, Los Angeles, and Washington D.C.'s Dulles International Airport.

Today, United Airlines is one of the top major carriers servicing over 200 destinations in 30 countries. The subsidiary of UAL Corporation serves the world's four largest markets: U.S. domestic, Asia, Europe, and Latin America. United maintains five major hubs along with its sister marketing brand- partner airline, United Express, which consists of a number of smaller regional airlines, serving smaller community cities from United's hubs in the United States.

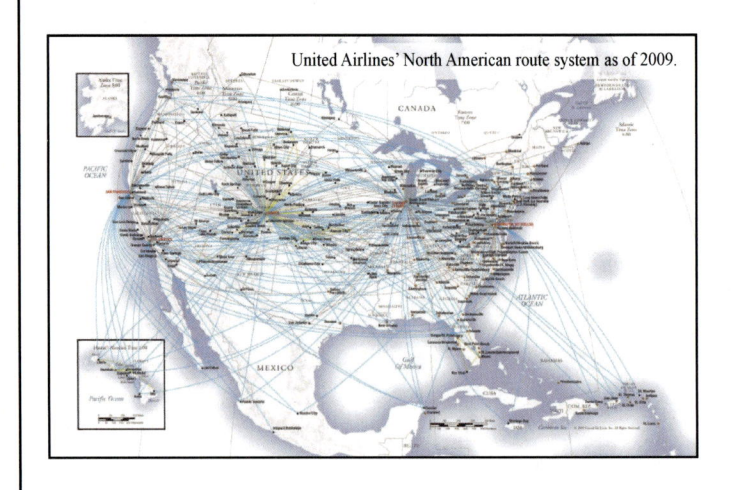

United Airlines' North American route system as of 2009.

United's premier member lounge, Red Carpet Club, is located at 28 major airports with 35 locations worldwide.

Mileage Plus, United's frequent flyer program and second largest loyalty program in the world, launched on May 6, 1981 with over 54 million members throughout the globe.

UNITED AIRLINES

Boeing 777-200ER

Boeing 757-200

Facts & Figures

Founded..	1926 (as Varney Air Lines)
Callsign...	"UNITED"
IATA designator................................	UA
IATA accounting................................	016
ICAO designator................................	UAL
Frequent flyer program.....................	Mileage Plus
Fleet count..	409

(55) A319-100, (97) A320-200, (30), B737-300, (16) B737-500, (27)B747-400, (97) B757-200, (35) B767-300ER, (19) B777-200, (33) B777-200ER

Total destinations.............................	210
Total countries served.....................	28
Parent company................................	UAL Corporation : NASDAQ: UAUA
Headquarters....................................	Chicago, IL
In-flight magazine.............................	*Hemispheres*
Member lounge.................................	Red Carpet Club
Primary hub(s)..................................	Denver, Los Angeles, Chicago/O'Hare, Washington, D.C. / Dulles
Secondary hub(s)..............................	San Francisco
Brands...	United Express
Global Alliance..................................	Star Alliance
Approximate number of employees....	50,000
Website...	united.com
Toll-free reservations.......................	1-800-241-6522
Route structure.................................	Hub-and-spoke
Reservations computer system.........	Apollo
Reservations call center locations.....	Chicago, Honolulu, Detroit, Mumbai, India; and Manila, Philippines.
Boeing customer code......................	22

61

US AIRWAYS

Airbus A330-300

Photo courtesy of Alan Pingstone

The nation's fourth largest airline and co-launch customer of the Boeing 737-300 traces its roots to Pittsburgh-based All American Aviation Company in May 1939, providing air mail services to the Ohio River Valley and Allegheny Mountain Region of Pennsylvania., West Virginia, and Eastern Ohio. The largest portions of each route lay in the mountainous region and required flights to operate during the Mid-Atlantic's worst weather over difficult terrain.

All American Aviation first took to the skies with a fleet of five bright scarlet Stinson Reliant SR-10 aircraft. Three planes made this inaugural flight on May 12, 1939, where the first official airmail pickup flight occurred. On March 7, 1949, All American Airways was born, scheduling passenger services on a fleet of eleven Douglas DC-3 aircraft. The company was again renamed Allegheny Airlines in 1953, with the launch of their first seven o'clock A.M. flight from Washington National Airport to Pittsburgh, with several scheduled stops in-between.

The Allegheny Commuter network was formed in 1967, when Allegheny, still a regional airline servicing smaller communities, encountered financial problems whilst deciding how to better serve these smaller cities. Leslie O. Barnes, former Allegheny president, responded by purchasing new, faster aircraft such as the Beech 99 turboprop; a cost-efficient, 15-passenger airplane produced by the Beech Craft Company of Wichita, Kansas (known today as Hawker Beechcraft Corporation). Allegheny's response opened doors for the ambitious, expanding carrier, which allowed the opportunity to grow far from where it had previously been. Allegheny expanded progressively, following the acquisition of Indianapolis-based Lake Central Airlines in 1968 and Utica, New York-based Mohawk Airlines in 1972. At that time, Allegheny operated a fleet of 108 aircraft consisting of McDonnell-Douglas DC-9s, BAC-111s, and Convair 550s. But with the expansion came growing pains: the newly expanded airline had earned the nickname "Agony Air" due to customer dissatisfaction with the carrier's overall performance. Allegheny's agreement with Henson Airlines, the immediate predecessor to today's US Airways Express carrier, Piedmont Airlines, provided service under the Allegheny Commuter brand, is generally regarded as the industry's first code-share agreement, which is commonplace in the ever-changing industry today.

On October 28, 1979 Allegheny became USAir, following the passage of the Airline Deregulation Act of 1978, which enabled the airline to expand its route network into the Southeastern United States, to form to become one of the largest carriers in the Northeastern United States and sixth largest airline in the world, as measured by number of passengers carried. Next to follow into USAir's flight path was Empire Airlines of New York, operating a fleet of brightly colored yellow, orange, and red Fokker F-28 aircraft. Empire's ambitious publically-owned life ended in 1985 when Piedmont Airlines, a former mega-carrier and forerunner to a merger partner with USAir, announced its $41.6 billion bid on the carrier. The partnership began in 1986, giving USAir instant access to Piedmont's major gateways in the Northeast.

USAir gained several California routes following the acquisition of San Diego-based Pacific Southwest Airlines (PSA) in April of 1988. Several of PSA's vividly colored McDonnell-Douglas and British Aerospace aircraft, all of their renowned painted-on smiles, were converted to USAir's silver, red, maroon, and burgundy color scheme. The airline launched several marketing advertisements to announce the historical

US AIRWAYS

merger with the slogan: "Smile, PSA is now USAir!" reflecting the once famed West Coast airline's unique and well-recognized paint scheme feature.

Perhaps one of the most memorable mergers of USAir's history occurred on August 5, 1989, the day after Winston-Salem, North Carolina based Piedmont Airlines flew its final flight, ending a legacy that began in the early 1960s, when Piedmont and USAir joined forces to form a larger, more customer-driven airline. Following the merger, USAir gained all of Piedmont's outstanding assets which included its former destinations and hubs and maintenance and ground facilities in the Northeast, and a fleet of Boeing 727, 737, 767, and Fokker 100 aircraft. The newer, expanded USAir unveiled a new color scheme, maintaining their polished metal silver body. While retaining hubs in Pittsburgh, Philadelphia, Cleveland, and Indianapolis, the airline added Piedmont's Charlotte, Dayton, Baltimore-Washington, and Syracuse hubs to the already growing network.

The next major change for the airline with the most impressive and colorful history, occurred on November 6, 1996, when USAir changed its name to US Airways. Along with the name-change, the re-branding included major changes to the airline's overall image, which led to the introduction of a new corporate logo, reflecting modified silhouette-type version of the American Flag, and undergone a complete makeover, while incorporating a brand new paint scheme for its entire fleet of over 400 aircraft. The airline giant's final merger of the century occurred on May 18, 2005, following major financial struggles including filing for Chapter 11 bankruptcy protection and cutting costs dramatically, when US Airways and Phoenix-based America West Airlines finalized merger agreements to retain the US Airways name, while retiring the America West brand name. As a very strong and financially stable carrier of the Western United States with hubs in Phoenix and Las Vegas, America West Airlines began its first flight on August 1, 1983, from Phoenix Sky Harbor Airport with just three airplanes to four cities, and grew to become the nation's eighth largest airline with over 14,000 employees.

US Airways has acquired some of history's most significant airline carriers, and operates today as the nation's largest, low-fare, full service airline with flights to more than 200 cities worldwide, including coast-to-coast service across the U.S., including Alaska and Hawaii, and Internationally serves a multitude of destinations in Canada, Mexico, Central America, the Caribbean, and Europe. The airline, identified on the New York Stock Exchange (NYSE) as LCC for "Low-Cost Carrier", operates over 3,100 flights a day and maintains hub locations at Charlotte-Douglas International Airport in North Carolina, Philadelphia, and Phoenix with several key focus cities. The airline operates the US Airways Shuttle which provides hourly service between major Northeastern markets, and US Airways Express, branded as its main regional service, which is operated and contracted by subsidiary airline companies such as Air Wisconsin, Chautauqua Airlines, Colgan Air, Mesa Airlines, PSA, Piedmont, Republic Airways, and Trans States Airlines.

US Airways Club locations total more than 20 locations at over 20 airports.

US AIRWAYS Club

US AIRWAYS

N828AW: This Airbus A-319, in classic America West Airlines livery, is one of four "heritage" paint schemes to commemorate each one of its predecessors.

Airbus A-320

Facts & Figures

Founded	1939 (as All American Aviation)
Callsign	"CACTUS"
IATA designator	US
IATA accounting	037
ICAO designator	AWE
Frequent flyer program	Dividend Miles
Fleet count	353 (+153)

(93) A319-100 (+9 orders), (74) A320-200 (+51 orders), (33) A321-200 (+33 orders), (15) A330-200, (9) A330-300, (0) A350-800 (+18 orders), (0)+4 A350-900 (+4 orders), (30) 737-300, (40) 737-400, + (39) 757-200, (10) 767-200

Total destinations	231
Total countries served	30
Parent company	US Airways Group: NYSE: LCC
Headquarters	Tempe, AZ
In-flight magazine	*US Airways Magazine* (formerly *Attaché Magazine*)
Member lounge	US Airways Club
Primary hub(s)	Charlotte, Philadelphia, and Phoenix
Secondary hub(s)	LGA, LAS, BOS, DCA
Subsidiaries	Piedmont Airlines and PSA Airlines
Brands	US Airways Shuttle and US Airways Express
Global Alliance	Star Alliance
Approximate number of employees	36,600
Website	usairways.com
Toll-free reservations	1-800-428-4322
Route structure	Hub-and-spoke
Reservations computer system	Shares (Division of Amadeus)
Reservations call center locations	Winston-Salem, NC; Tempe, AZ; Reno, and Liverpool, UK
Boeing customer code	B7

65

USA 3000
AIRLINES

Airbus A320-200

USA3000 AIRLINES

A sister company to the Apple Leisure Group, headquartered in Newtown Square, Pennsylvania, USA3000 Airlines operates a fleet of new, state-of-the-art Airbus A320 aircraft. The airline services 20 destinations in the United States, Mexico, the Dominican Republic, and Jamaica. Exclusive charter flight operations began in 2001 when the carrier was officially certified as an FAA Part 121 carrier, with just two aircraft serving Philadelphia, Newark, Hartford, Columbus, and later Chicago, with the addition of a third aircraft in May 2002.

USA3000 Airlines' first destinations were Cancun, Mexico and Punta Cana, Dominican Republic. The inaugural flight on December 28, 2001 flew from Philadelphia to Cancun. Scheduled international passenger service soon followed in 2002, after which the airline added domestic routes, expanding service to Fort Myers, St. Petersburg, and Fort Lauderdale-Hollywood in 2003. In the years to come, rising oil and fuel prices and an unstable economy necessitated the closing of some Florida markets in an ongoing effort to maintain the airline's success. Flights were retained to Fort Myers, as the most profitable revenue-building gateway, and service to St. Petersburg was soon re-opened.

Today's USA3000 Airlines prides itself on achieving some of the most prestigious performance recognition awards in the industry. The airline was voted one of the top five domestic carriers by readers of *Travel+Leisure Magazine* and one of the top ten by *Condé Naste Traveler* Magazine. Each Airbus A320 aircraft is configured to offer spacious, comfortable seating to accommodate 168 passengers. The A320 was selected by the airline for its environmentally-friendly qualities, as the aircraft burn less fuel, produce less noise, and generate fewer emissions than most any other aircraft, and its range allows for nonstop flights, making convenience a key of the customer-focused operation. In order to improve the quality of its service, USA3000 continually surveys hundreds of thousands of passengers upon completion of their trips. The airline values its customers' opinions, and provides complimentary nonalcoholic beverages, "friendly service", free headsets and inflight entertainment (including nine channels of audio entertainment), more legroom, and boasted a 93% on-time performance record for 2008. The carrier offers children a free tour of the flight deck, kids' menu item selections—*"Sky Picnic"*, and 'First Flight' certificates available for first-time fliers, a rare incentive that was once widely available in the primitive days of airline travel.

Similar to most airlines' buy-on-board meal options, USA3000 offers meals that are "healthy and carefully selected by experts for their quality and nutritional value." The carrier's latest premier guest loyalty program, Preferred Perks, launched in 2009, provides paid members with a dedicated check-in lane at the airport ticket counter, entrance to airport security checkpoints when available, first choice of preferred seating, and priority baggage handling. In order to commit to their "Experience the Difference" marketing strategy, the airline, along with sister companies Apple Vacations, which has been in existence for over 40 years, and Amstar Destination Management, appoint representatives to greet their passengers upon arrival in international destinations in the Caribbean and Mexico, to provide assistance with hotel transfers, as well as return transportation to the airport on the date of departure.

USA3000 recognizes Amstar as an extension of the carrier's "friendly service in the sky" with a "friendly face at your resort." The hotel division of the Apple Leisure Group, AMResorts, and Apple Vacations, are all

USA3000 AIRLINES

affiliated with USA3000 Airlines which is owned by Brendan Airways, LLC, and maintains focus cities in St. Louis, Pittsburgh, Detroit, Chicago, Milwaukee, and Baltimore/Washington International Airport.

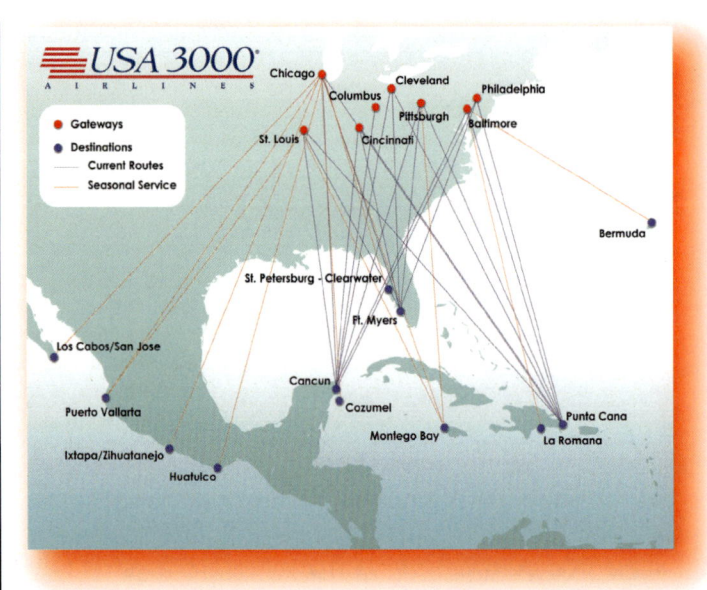

USA 3000's route system as of 2009.

USA3000 Airlines uniformed agents pose proudly at Detroit's Metropolitan Wayne County Airport.

USA3000 Airlines' Preferred Perkes program debuted in 2009 to offer its paid members an incentive to several *"perks"* on the ground and in the air.

USA3000 AIRLINES

Airbus A-320

Airbus A-320

Facts & Figures

Founded	2001
Callsign	"GETAWAY"
IATA designator	U5
IATA accounting	336
ICAO designator	GWY
Paid membership program	Preferred Perks
Fleet count	11

(11) Airbus A320-200

Total destinations	20
Total countries served	5
Parent company	Brendan Airways, LLC (private ownership)
Headquarters	Newton Square, PA
In-flight magazine	*Roam*
Member lounge	N/A
Primary hub(s)	N/A
Focus cities	Mexico and the Caribbean
Subsidiaries	N/A
Global Alliance	N/A
Approximate number of employees	700
Website	usa3000.com
Toll-free reservations	1-877-872-3000
Route structure	Point-to-point
Reservations computer system	Radixx
Reservations call center locations	Newton Square, PA

69

virgin america

Airbus A320

VIRGIN AMERICA

California-based Virgin America launched service on August 8, 2007 and is aimed to provide low-fare, high quality service with "brand new planes, attractive fares, topnotch service, and a host of fun" including innovative amenities that is said to reinvent domestic air travel. The airline's base of operations is San Francisco International Airport's "ultra-modern" International Terminal. In less than two years since its first flight, Virgin America had introduced service to its ninth destination in April 2009 -- John Wayne Airport, Orange County-Santa Ana, California; to add to its existing eight cities across the U.S. including San Francisco, Los Angeles, New York's JFK International Airport, San Diego, Washington D.C.'s Dulles International Airport, Las Vegas, Seattle/Tacoma, and Boston.

Being among the newest start-up airlines in the United States, Virgin America traces its roots to early 2004, when London, England based branded venture capital Virgin Group LTD, announced its intensions to launch a new low-fare airline to be based in the United States and naming it "Virgin USA", to coincide with other Virgin airline brands such as Virgin Atlantic Airways, Virgin Blue, Virgin Nigeria, and Virgin Galactic; but have it operate independently apart from other Virgin branded airlines to comply with U.S. Federal Law. Virgin USA's expectations to begin service in 2005 were delayed due to detriments in locating U.S. investors. After changing its name to Virgin America, the airline secured its primary funds and awaited the lengthy approval process of its application of certification. After over one year of struggles with political and national aviation labor union opposition, their long-awaited certificate to operate as a scheduled U.S. passenger air carrier was finally approved in March, 2007; thence after final preparations, the airline began passenger ticket sales in July of that year. The airline, whose partial capital stock through British entrepreneur Sir Richard Branson, is 75% owned by VAI Partners LLC and remaining 25% owned by Virgin Group, which also licenses the Virgin brand name to the airline. The U.S. based carrier operates a consistent fleet of Airbus A319 and A320 aircraft and offers dual-class service on all flights. Both cabins, First Class and Main Cabin, feature an impressive innovative mood lighting system with 12 shades that adapt to outside light, in which Virgin America was the first American carrier to pioneer this element on domestic flights, and is said to create a more pleasant and relaxing environment for the passengers and crew. All custom-designed leather seats are equipped with 110-volt power outlets, USB and RJ-45 Ethernet jacks near every seat, Panasonic Aviation's personal in-flight entertainment (IFE) system with a nine-inch video touch-screen concept named *"Red"*, and qwerty keyboard/remote controls installed on every seatback. Main Cabin Select, the airline's premium economy product, is located in the Main Cabin seating area and features larger seats located in the emergency exit rows and bulkhead area, featuring 38 inches of seat pitch and designated overhead compartments.

In addition to comfort in mind, the airline launched a fleet-wide inflight internet service in the Spring of 2009, complimenting customers' on-demand access to over 25 films, 18 channels of live TV, videogames, seat-to-seat chat, interactive maps, over 3,000 MP3 library with the ability to create your own playlist, kids' entertainment section with parental controls, and world's first food and drink ordering system at the "touch-of-a-button." Virgin America First Class service, attractively adorned with large two across plush white premium leather seats and "Virgin-red" oversized pillows, features 55 inches of pitch and 28 inches wide, with a 165-degree incline while the Main Cabin features 38-inch pitch seats. Since its inaugural launch, the carrier has not only been

VIRGIN AMERICA

identified as the first commercial passenger airline to be accepted into U.S. EPA Climate Leaders Program, but has earned awards and accolades such as Best Domestic Airline in *Condé Nast Traveler*'s 2008 Readers' Choice Awards, Best U.S. Business/First Class in 2008 *Condé Nast Traveler* Business Travel Poll, Number one in Zagat's 2007 and 2008 Global Airlines survey of 7,500 frequent fliers for quality in First/Business Class and was rated second for quality in Coach among domestic carriers, and in 2008 was presented with *TravelZoo*'s 'TZoo Award' for best travel innovator.

The airline's loyalty program, Elevate, operates on a "dollars-spent" versus actual air miles flown concept, being the first commercial U.S. airline to operate a frequent flyer program without awards redeemed on a point or mileage accrual scale.

Virgin America's destinations as of 2009.

The airline's one-of-a-kind mood-lit cabins offer a relaxing ambiance and biological-clock-adjusting friendly environment.

Elevate, Virgin America's loyalty program, offers award travel incentives based on dollars spent versus the traditional air miles flown or points earned system.

elevate
IT'S DIFFERENT UP HERE.

72

VIRGIN AMERICA

Airbus A-320

Airbus A-320

Facts & Figures

Founded	2004
Callsign	"REDWOOD"
IATA designator	VX
IATA accounting	984
ICAO designator	VRD
Frequent flyer program	Elevate
Fleet count	28

(10) Airbus A-319 (+7 orders), (18) Airbus A-320 (+3 orders)

Total destinations	9
Total countries served	1
Parent company	75% VAI Partners, LLC; 25% Virgin Group (private)
Headquarters	Burlingame, CA
In-flight magazine	N/A
Member lounge	N/A
Primary hub(s)	San Francisco
Secondary hub(s)	N/A
Subsidiaries	N/A
Global Alliance	N/A
Approximate number of employees	1,400
Website	virginamerica.com
Toll-free reservations	1-877-359-8474
Route structure	Hub-and-spoke
Reservations computer system	aiRES
Reservations call center locations	Burlingame, CA

73

Wings Over America

REGIONAL AIRLINES
AND
BRAND NAMES

Air Wisconsin • AmericanConnection • American Eagle

Founded in 1965 and based in Appleton, Wisconsin, Air Wisconsin Airlines Corporation is the largest privately-held regional airline in the United States. The airline is operated under the brand name of US Airways Express and also provides ground handling support for other carriers. Air Wisconsin schedules 500 departures per day to 69 cities in 26 states and two Canadian provinces with hubs at PHL, DCA, and LGA. The fleet consists of (70) Canadair CRJ-200LR jet aircraft.

IATA: ZW / 303 **Callsign**: "AIR WISCONSIN" **ICAO**: AWI airwis.com

Bombardier CRJ-200LR

AmericanConnection

Operated by Chautauqua Airlines, AmericanConnection is the brand name and a regional affiliate of American Airlines, Inc. at its Saint Louis Lambert International Airport hub. Operating under the **one**world alliance, AmericanConnection serves 23 destinations with over 180 flights a day. The Indianapolis-based airline's fleet consists of (15) Embraer ERJ-140 aircraft with a seating capacity of 44 passengers.

IATA: AX / 414 **Callsign**: "CHAUTAUQUA" **ICAO**: CHQ flychautauqua.com

Embraer ERJ-140

American Eagle

Founded in 1984 as a wholly-owned subsidiary of Fort Worth, Texas-based AMR Corporation, American Eagle is recognized as the world's largest regional airline system. The airline's hubs are located at ORD, DFW, STL, LAX, SJU, MIA, BOS, LGA, and RDU. Together with San Juan-based Executive Airlines, the carrier operates a fleet of 270 aircraft which consists of: (25) Bombardier CRJ-700, (32) Embraer ERJ-135, (59) ERJ-140, (112) ERJ-145, (27) ATR 72-200/210, and (12) ATR 72-200/212-A; with over 1,800 flights per day seving 159 cities across the U.S.A., Canada, Mexico, and the Caribbean.

IATA: MQ / 001 **Callsign**: "EAGLE FLIGHT" **ICAO**: EGF aa.com

Bombardier CRJ-700

Atlantic Southeast Airlines (ASA) • Cape Air • Chautauqua Airlines

Bombardier CRJ-900

A wholly-owned subsidiary of SkyWest, Inc., Atlanta-based Atlantic Southeast Airlines was founded in 1979 and operates under the Delta Connection brand name. The regional airline serves over 105 destinations throughout the United States, Canada, Mexico, and the Caribbean utilizing a fleet of 160 jet aircraft consisting of: (112) Bombardier CRJ-200ER, (38) CRJ-700ER, and (10) CRJ-900ER. Hubs are located in Cincinnati and Atlanta.

IATA: EV / 862   **Callsign**: "ACEY"   **ICAO**: ASQ   flyasa.com

Cessna 402-C

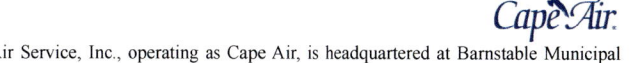

Hyannis Air Service, Inc., operating as Cape Air, is headquartered at Barnstable Municipal Airport in Barnstable, Massachusetts and operates scheduled passenger services in the Northeast, Florida, the Caribbean, Mid-Atlantic States, and Micronesia. Flights in Florida and Micronesia are operated as Continental Connection flights through a code share partnership with Continental Airlines. Flights between Hyannis and Nantucket, Massachusetts, are operated under the Nantucket Airlines brand, a wholly-owned subsidiary of Cape Air. The airline serves 29 destinations and operates a fleet consisting of (56) Cessna 402C, and (2) ATR 42-320.

IATA: 9K / 306   **Callsign**: "C AIR"   **ICAO**: KAP   flycapeair.com

Embraer ERJ-170

Founded on May 3, 1973, Chautauqua Airlines, Inc., a subsidiary of Republic Airways Holdings based in Indianapolis, Indiana, operates scheduled passenger services with more than 460 flights daily to 68 airports in 27 states, Washington, D.C. and Canada through feeder services under the names AmericanConnection for American Airlines, Continental Express for Continental Airlines, Delta Connection for Delta Air Lines, Midwest Connect for Midwest Airlines, United Express for United Airlines, and US Airways Express for US Airways.

IATA: RP / 363   **Callsign**: "CHAUTAUQUA"   **ICAO**: CHQ   flychautauqua.com

Colgan Air • Comair • CommutAir

COLGAN AIR

Founded in 1991, Colgan Air, Inc., a fully certificated regional airline subsidiary of Pinnacle Airlines Corp. headquartered in Manassas, Virginia, has been operating as US Airways Express since 1999 and now serves over 50 cities in 15 U.S. states and Canada as a feeder for US Airways Express, United Express, and Continental Connection. Colgan Air's major hubs are located at LGA, BOS, IAD, EWR, and IAH. The Colgan Air fleet consists of (34) Saab 340B and (14) Bombardier Q400 aircraft.

IATA: 9L / 426   **Callsign**: "COLGAN"   **ICAO**: CJC   colganair.com

Bombardier Q400

Comair

Comair, one of the world's largest regional airlines founded in 1977, is a wholly-owned subsidiary of Delta Air Lines, Inc. and operates as part of the Delta Connection system. The regional carrier is based in Cincinnati, Ohio with hubs in Cincinnati and New York-JFK. The airline operates 530 flights a day to approximately 70 cities throughout the United States and Canada. Comair serves Delta's major hubs in Atlanta and Cincinnati and has a concentrated focus on major Northeast markets of New York's John F. Kennedy International Airport, LaGuardia Airport, Washington D.C.'s Reagan National Airport, and Boston's Logan International Airport. The Comair fleet consists of (104) Bombardier CRJ-100, (15) CRJ-700, and (14) CRJ-900 aircraft.

IATA: OH / 886   **Callsign**: "COMAIR"   **ICAO**: COM   comair.com

Bombardier CRJ-900

CommutAir

Owned by Champlain Enterprises, Inc., Cleveland, Ohio-based CommutAir operates under the brand name of Continental Connection for Continental Airlines, with its main bases at Cleveland Hopkins International Airport and Newark Liberty International Airport. Founded in 1989, the regional carrier serves destinations mainly in the Midwest and Northeastern United States. The CommutAir fleet consists of (16) Bombardier Dash 8 Q200 aircraft.

IATA: C5 / 841   **Callsign**: "COMMUTAIR"   **ICAO**: UCA   commutair.com

Bombardier Q200

Compass Airlines • Continental Connection • Continental Express

Embraer ERJ-175LR

Compass Airlines

Compass Airlines, based in Chantilly, Virginia and founded in 2006, is a subsidiary of Delta Air Lines that began flying a single Bombardier CRJ200LR aircraft under the Northwest Airlink brand between Minneapolis/St. Paul and Washington, D.C. on May 2, 2007. Its main hub is Minneapolis/St. Paul International Airport. On August 21, 2007, it began flying two Embraer 175 76-passenger aircraft, with a planned fleet of 36 aircraft by December, 2008. The fleet consists of (36) Embraer 175LR aircraft.

IATA: CP / 003   **Callsign**: "COMPASS ROSE"   **ICAO**: CPZ   compassairline.com

Beech 1900D Twin Turboprop

Continental Connection

Operated by Cape Air, Colgan Air, CommutAir, and Gulfstream International Airlines, the Continental Connection brand name operates service marketed exclusively by Continental Airlines. All Continental Connection service is provided using a total of 153 turboprop aircraft including (2) ATR-42 and (54) Cessna 402 aircraft operated by Cape Air, (14) Bombardier Dash 8-Q400 and (42) Saab 340B operated by Colgan Air, (15) Bombardier Dash 8-Q200 operated by CommutAir, and (26) Raytheon Beech 1900D aircraft operated by Gulfstream International Airlines. As with mainline Continental Airlines, the brand name is also part of the SkyTeam Alliance and passengers may accrue mileage with the OnePass frequent flyer program.

Bombardier CRJ-200ER

Continental Express

Continental Express is the operating name brand of a number of independently owned regional airlines providing regional jet feeder service in association with Continental Airlines. Currently, two carriers operate under the Continental Express brand name: ExpressJet and Chautauqua Airlines. Continental Express offers service to approximately 150 destinations in the United States, Canada, Mexico, and the Caribbean, from Continental's hubs in Houston, Newark, and Cleveland. ExpressJet Airlines is the only regional airline operating exclusively as a Continental Express carrier.

79

Delta Connection • Delta Shuttle • Era Aviation

DELTA CONNECTION

The Delta Connection brand name consists of several regional airlines which operates as a feeder service for mainline Delta Air Lines at several Delta cities throughout North America. The regional airlines which fly in Delta Connection colors are: Comair, Compass Airlines, Mesaba Airlines, Atlantic Southeast Airlines (ASA), Chautauqua Airlines, Freedom Airlines, Pinnacle Airlines, Shuttle America, and SkyWest Airlines. SkyMiles benefits apply to travel on all Delta Connection carriers and are also a part of the SkyTeam alliance.

Bombardier CRJ-900

DELTA SHUTTLE

The Pan Am Shuttle, which ceased operations in 1991, was sold to Delta Air Lines in September of that year and became the Delta Shuttle, the airline's brand name which services competitive Northeast business traveler-related markets between Boston's Logan International Airport and New York's La Guardia Airport, and separate service between Washington D.C.'s Reagan National and New York's La Guardia Airport. The Delta Shuttle operates MD-88 aircraft owned by mainline Delta, and Embraer 175 aircraft operated by Shuttle America. Delta Shuttle offers First and Economy Class service providing snacks and complimentary wine and beer.

McDonnell-Douglas MD-88

Era

Era Aviation was established and began operations in 1948 when the first commercial helicopter to Alaska to work on a mapping contract for the US Government. Scheduled passenger services began in May 1983. A part of of The Frontier Alaska Company, along with Frontier Flying Service and Hageland Aviation, the combined partnership make up the largest carrier in the State of Alaska. Based at Anchorage's Ted Stevens International Airport, the airline operates a network of services from their home base as part of Alaska Airlines Partnerships. The fleet consists of (4) Bombardier Dash 8 Q106 and (3) 3 Beechcraft 1900D aircraft serving Anchorage, Aniak, Barrow, Bethel, Cordova, Emmonak, Fairbanks, Homer, Kenai, Kodiak, St. Mary's, Valdez, Alaska.

IATA: 7H / 808   **Callsign**: "ERA"   **ICAO**: ERH   flyera.com

Bombardier Dash 8 Q106

80

ExpressJet Airlines • Freedom Airlines • Frontier Alaska

EXPRESSJET

The largest operator of the Embraer Regional Jet (ERJ), Houston-based ExpressJet Airlines traces its roots to 1987 when a group of smaller commuter airlines, including Bar Harbor Airlines, Provincetown-Boston Airlines (PBA), Rocky Mountain Air, and Indiana-based Britt Airways, were acquired by Continental Airlines and rebranded under the Continental Express name. Sharing hubs at Cleveland Hopkins International Airport, Houston's Intercontinental Airport, and Newark Liberty International Airport, ExpressJet Airlines serves 151 destinations with a fleet of (140) Embraer ERJ-145, (104) Embraer ERJ-145XR, of which 214 aircraft operate for Continental Express, and 30 fly for its corporate division for charter services.

Embraer ERJ 145

IATA: XE / 477   **Callsign**: "JET   **ICAO**: BTA   expressjet.com

FREEDOM AIRLINES

The launch customer of the Bombardier CRJ-900 which began operations in October 2002, Freedom Airlines, part of Mesa Air Group, initiated service under the America West Express brand name for America West Airlines, based at Phoenix Sky Harbor International Airport. Today, the airline flies under the Delta Connection brand for Delta Air Lines and operates a fleet of (25) Embraer ERJ-145 aircraft and serves 24 destinations, retaining their hub at New York's JFK International Airport.

Embraer ERJ-145LR

IATA: F8   **Callsign**: "FREEDOM AIR"   **ICAO**: FRL   mesa-air.com

Frontier Alaska

Frontier Flying Service, Inc., operates as Fairbanks, Alaska-based Frontier Alaska, owned by parent company HoTH's Air Group Holdings, combined with Hageland Aviation Services and Era Aviation. The three carriers combined employ approximately 700 workers, and are in codeshare partnership with Seattle-based Alaska Airlines, Inc. and serves over 100 destinations within the State of Alaska, operating a fleet of (12) Raytheon Beech BE-1900-C and (11) Piper PA-31-50 twin turboprop aircraft.

Raytheon Beech BE-1900C

IATA: 2F / 517   **Callsign**: "FRONTIER AIR"   **ICAO**: FTA   frontierflying.com

81

go! • go! Express • GoJet Airlines

Based in Honolulu, *go!*, "Hawaii's Low Fare Airline", is a regional brand of Phoenix-based Mesa Airlines, subsidiary of Mesa Air Group. The airline's fleet of Bombardier CRJ-200 serves eight destinations within the Hawaiian Islands, operated by Mesa Airlines, and began service on June 9, 2006. The airline had formed agreements with Honolulu-based Island Air to operate its flights under the *go!* Express sub-brand. The airline offers a frequent flyer program, *go!* Miles, and its very own inflight magazine, "*Iflygo*".

IATA: YV / 533   **Callsign**: "AIR SHUTTLE"   **ICAO**: ASH   iflygo.com

Bombardier CRJ-200

go! Express is operated by Honolulu-based Island Air, and is a brand name of Hawaii's *go!* operated by Mesa Airlines. *go!* Express operates flights from Honolulu, Kahului, Hilo, Kona, and Lihue to smaller Hawaiian airports which include Kapalua and Hoolehua.

IATA: WP / 347   **Callsign**: "MOKU"   **ICAO**: MKU   iflygo.com / islandair.com

Bombardier Dash 8-100

St. Louis-based GoJet Airlines is a wholly owned subsidiary of Trans States Holdings, and operates under the United Express brand name. The airline's fleet consists of (19) 66-passenger Bombardier CRJ-702ER aircraft, offering three classes of service: First, Economy Plus ("explus"), and Economy. The airline shares hubs with mainline United Airlines at Denver International Airport and Washington, D.C. Dulles International Airport. GoJet Airlines serves as an intricate part of United's feeder operations with crew bases in St. Louis and Chicago's O'Hare International Airport.

IATA: G7 / 573   **Callsign**: "LINDBERGH"   **ICAO**: GJS   gojetairlines.com

Bombardier CRJ-700

Great Lakes Airlines • Gulfstream International Airlines • Hageland Aviation Services

Raytheon Beechcraft 1900D

Cheyenne, Wyoming-based Great Lakes Airlines serves as a regional airline operating both scheduled and charter air services. With hubs at Denver International Airport, Kansas City International Airport, Phoenix Sky Harbor International Airport, Lambert-St. Louis International Airport, Billings Logan International Airport, LA/ Ontario International Airport, Milwaukee General Mitchell International Airport, and Albuquerque International Sunport, Great Lakes Airlines' fleet consists of (6) Embraer EMB 1200ER Brasilia and (31) Raytheon Beechcraft 1900D aircraft, and serves 66 destinations throughout the U.S.

IATA: ZK / 846 **Callsign**: "LAKES AIR" **ICAO**: GLA flygreatlakes.com

Raytheon Beechcraft 1900D

Founded in 1988, Gulfstream International Airlines operates scheduled and charter services to Florida, the Bahamas, and the Caribbean. Its scheduled services operate under the Continental Connection brand name for Continental Airlines. The airline's main base is Fort Lauderdale-Hollywood International Airport, with hubs at Miami International Airport, Palm Beach International Airport, and Tampa International Airport—operating a fleet of (23) Raytheon Beech 1900D aircraft.

IATA: 3M / 449 **Callsign**: "GULF FLIGHT" **ICAO**: GFT gulfstreamair.com

Raytheon Beechcraft 1900C

Founded in 1981 and based in Anchorage, Hageland Aviation Services serves nine destinations in Alaska and operates statewide charter services. The airline is part of Frontier Alaska Company and maintains its main hub at Wiley Post-Will Rogers Memorial Airport, Barrow, Alaska. Its fleet of 40 aircraft consists of: (2) Beech 1900C Airliner, (1) Beech 1900C Cargo, (4) Reims/ Cessna F406, (14) Cessna 208B Caravan, (16) Cessna 207 "Sled", (2) Cessna 206, and (1) Cessna 180 aircraft.

IATA: H6 **Callsign**: "HAGELAND" **ICAO**: HAG hageland.com

83

Horizon Air • Island Air • Lynx Aviation

Horizon Air

Founded in 1981 when its inaugural flight was launched from Seattle to Yakima, Washington, Seattle-based Horizon Air serves as a sister carrier to Alaska Airlines, both part of Alaska Air Group. Horizon Air is the nation's eighth largest regional airline, serving 48 cities in the United States, Canada, and Mexico. The airline's fleet of nearly 60 aircraft consists of (37) Bombardier Dash 8 Q-400 twin turboprop and (18) Bombardier CRJ-700 jet aircraft.

IATA: QX / 481   **Callsign**: "HORIZON AIR"   **ICAO**: QXE   horizonair.com

Bombardier Dash 8 Q-400

Island Air

What began in 1980 as Princeville Airways and later sold to Aloha Air Group, parent company of Aloha Airlines, the small inter-island commuter was renamed Aloha IslandAir in May 1987 and served as a subsidiary of Aloha Airlines which ceased operations in 2008. On May 11, 2004 the airline was renamed Hawaii Island Air following the sale of the carrier to Gavarnie Holding, LLC and conducts business under the name "Island Air". Based in Honolulu on the Hawaiian Island of Oahu, the airline flies 37 passenger (6) Bombardier Dash 8-100/200 aircraft to eight cities throughout the Hawaiian Islands.

IATA: WP / 347   **Callsign**: "MOKU"   **ICAO**: MKU   islandair.com

Bombardier Dash 8-102

Lynx Aviation

Denver-based Lynx Aviation, Inc. serves as a subsidiary and regional feeder service of Frontier Airlines operating from its Denver hub to a total of 15 destinations in the U.S. The airline was formed on September 6, 2006 and began passenger operations on December 7, 2007. Comparable to Frontier Airlines' wildlife themed tail fins, Lynx Aviation's fleet of (11) Bombardier Dash 8 Q-400 aircraft exhibits younger versions of animals from "Luke", the lynx kitten, to "Ginger", the baby red fox pup.

IATA: L4 / 422   **Callsign**: "SHASTA"   **ICAO**: SSX   frontierairlines.com

Bombardier Dash 8 Q400

Mesa Airlines • Mesaba Airlines • Midwest Connect

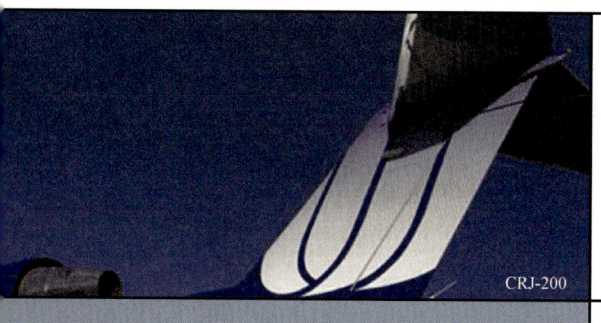

CRJ-200

A division of Mesa Air Group and operating as brand names such as US Airways Express from US Airways' hub airports in Phoenix, Las Vegas, and Charlotte, as United Express from United's hub cities in Denver, Washington D.C./Dulles, and Chicago/O'Hare, as Honolulu-based *go!*, "Hawaii's low fare airline", and as Delta Connection, via Freedom Airlines, Mesa Airlines operates a total of 163 aircraft ranging from Bombardier Canadair Regional Jet 900, 100/200, and 700ER to Embraer ERJ-145LR jets serving over 180 cities coast to coast.

IATA: YV / 533   **Callsign**: "AIR SHUTTLE"   **ICAO**: ASH   www.mesa-air.com

MESABA AIRLINES

Saab 340-B

Operating as Delta Connection, Eagan, Minnesota-based Mesaba Airlines operates under Mesaba Aviation, a wholly-owned subsidiary of Atlanta-based Delta Air Lines, Inc. The airline was founded in 1944 and became a codeshare partner of the former Republic Airlines in 1983 serving the airline's hub as its feeder service out of the Minneapolis/St. Paul International Airport. Following the merger with Republic Airlines and Northwest Orient in 1986, began serving as the Northwest AirLink brand name until the Northwest Airlines and Delta mega-merger in 2009. The airline serves 64 destinations with a fleet of 109 aircraft which include: (19) CRJ-200LR, (41) CRJ-900, and (49) Saab 340B aircraft. The main hub locations are in Minneapolis, Detroit, Memphis, Atlanta, and Salt Lake City.

IATA: XJ / 582   **Callsign**: "MESABA"   **ICAO**: MES   www.mesaba.com

MIDWEST CONNECT

Embraer 170 operated by Republic Airlines

Midwest Connect serves as the brand name for Midwest Airlines' sole regional airline subsidiary, operated by both Chautauqua and Republic Airlines. Midwest Connect operates a fleet of (24) Embraer aircraft – including E-135s, E-145s, and E-170 regional jet aircraft. Under an air services agreement, Chautauqua Airlines operates 37-passenger Embraer 135 aircraft and 50-passenger Embraer 145 aircraft, and Republic Airlines operates 76-passenger Embraer E-170 aircraft – all of which are painted in the Midwest Connect livery; serving 27 cities, including Cleveland, OH; Columbus, OH; Dayton, OH; Des Moines, IA; Flint, MI; Grand Rapids, MI; Green Bay, WI ; Indianapolis, IN; Louisville, KY; Madison, WI; Nashville, TN; and Pittsburgh, PA; from Milwaukee's General Mitchell International Airport.

Mokulele Airlines • PenAir • Piedmont Airlines

Mokulele Airlines

Founded in 1998 and based in Kalaoa on the Big Island of Hawaii, Mokulele Airlines operates scheduled inter-island flights (operated by Shuttle America throughout Hawaii), to Honolulu, Hilo, Kahului, Kona, and Lihue; and operating as Mokulele Express, operated by Mokulele Airlines, to Honolulu, Kahului, Kona, and Molokai. Fifty percent of the airline's shares are owned by Republic Airways Holdings. Mokulele offers its own preferred members lounge, Ali'i Lounge, and frequent flyer program, Ali'i Rewards. The carrier's fleet consists of (3) Embraer 170, (6) Cessna 208B Grand Caravan, and (1) Cessna 208B Super Cargomaster aircraft.

IATA: MW / 415   **Callsign**: "SPEEDBUGGY"   **ICAO**: BUG   mokuleleairlines.com

Embraer EMB-170

PenAir

PenAir, abbreviated for Peninsula Airways, is Alaska's second largest commuter regional airline, founded in 1955, operating an extensive scheduled and passenger and cargo services to 36 communities throughout Southwest Alaska, as well as charter and medical evacuation services. Its main base of operations is Ted Stevens Anchorage International Airport, with hubs in Dillingham, King Salmon, Cold Bay, and Unalaska Airport located on Amaknak Island in the Aleutian Islands, off the coast of Alaska. The airline's fleet consists of 40 single to twin engine turboprop aircraft.

IATA: KS / 339   **Callsign**: "PENINSULA"   **ICAO**: PEN   penair.com

Fairchild SA227-DC

Piedmont

Piedmont Airlines was founded as Henson Airlines in 1962, and currently serves as a wholly-owned subsidiary of the US Airways Group. The airline operates as US Airways Express from its Charlotte and Philadelphia hubs. Along with the name-change in 1993 from Henson to Piedmont, the original Piedmont name and logo was resurrected in order to preserve the US Airways predecessor which was merged into USAir in 1989. The airline operates 55 De Havilland Canada Dash 8-100 and 300 series aircraft, and serves 49 cities in the Eastern U.S.

IATA: US / 037   **Callsign**: "PIEDMONT"   **ICAO**: PDT   piedmont-airlines.com

De Havilland Canada DHC-8-311A Dash 8

Pinnacle Airlines • PSA Airlines • Republic Airlines

Bombardier CRJ-200 LR

Memphis-based Pinnacle Airlines was founded in February 1985 as Express Airlines One, when it began codesharing with the former Republic Airlines at its Memphis hub operating BAe Jetstream 31 and Saab 340 aircraft. The airline soon after expanded into Republic's Minneapolis/St.Paul market, progressively adding more aircraft and destinations to its growing network. When Northwest Airlines purchased Republic in 1986, the airline, who changed its name to Pinnacle on May 8, 2002, was rebranded as Northwest AirLink until 2009 when Delta Air Lines and Northwest merged; Pinnacle has since served as part of the Delta Connection network.

IATA: 9E / 430   **Callsign**: "FLAGSHIP"   **ICAO**: FLG   flypinnacle.com

Bombardier CRJ-200ER

Flying for the US Airways Express brand name, Vandalia, Ohio- based PSA Airlines operates an all-jet fleet of (35) Bombardier CRJ-200LR and (14) CRJ-700ER aircraft. The airline, wholly owned by US Airways Group, was established in 1979 as Vee Neal Airlines which operated Cessna 402 flights from Latrobe, Pennsylvania to Pittsburgh. The airline was renamed Jetstream International Airlines (JIA) in 1983, as was affiliated with now defunct Piedmont Airlines by 1985. JIA then began operating as Allegheny Commuter from USAir's Philadelphia hub, following the airline's acquisition of Piedmont in November, 1987. JIA was renamed PSA on November 1, 1995 in order to protect the trademark the defunct San Diego-based Pacific Southwest Airlines, once a large West Coast carrer that merged with USAir in 1988.

IATA: US / 037   **Callsign**: "BLUE STREAK"   **ICAO**: JIA   psaairlines.com

Embraer 175

A regional subsidiary of Indianapolis-based Republic Airways Holdings, Republic Airlines operates service as US Airways Express at US Airways' hubs in Philadelphia, Washington D.C. (DCA) and Charlotte Douglas International Airport, and as the Midwest Connect brand at Milwaukee's General Mitchell International Airport. The airline operates (18) Embraer 170 and (36) Embraer 175 jet aircraft and serves 52 airports in the United States and Canada.

IATA: RW / 052   **Callsign**: "BRICKYARD"   **ICAO**: RPA   flyrepublic.com

87

Shuttle America • SkyWest Airlines • Trans States Airlines

SHUTTLE AMERICA
A REPUBLIC AIRWAYS COMPANY

Founded in 1995, Shuttle America began operations on November 12, 1998 as a low-fare commuter airline headquartered primarily in Windsor Locks, Connecticut. Shuttle America began flying routes from Hartford to Buffalo advertising "super-low" $29 one way fares on 50 passenger Bombardier Dash 8-300 painted in a very patriotic paint scheme. Following rapid growth and publicity, the airline added Hanscom Field in Bedford, Massachusetts, 12 miles to the west of Boston's Logan International Airport, and Trenton, New York's La Guardia Airport, and Greensboro, North Carolina. In the spring of 2005, the airline was purchased by Republic Airways Holdings, and operates as United Express, Delta Connection, and Honolulu-based Mokulele Airlines. The fleet consists of (46) EMB E-170-100 and (12) EMB E-175 aircraft.

IATA: S5 / 919   **Callsign**: "MERCURY"   **ICAO**: TCF   shuttleamerica.com

Embraer 170

SkyWest AIRLINES

Founded in 1972, SkyWest Airlines is one of two subsidiaries of its parent company SkyWest, Inc. based in St. George, Utah. Operating under the Delta Connection and United Express brand names, SkyWest serves destinations throughout the United States, Canada, and Mexico from its Chicago, Los Angeles, San Francisco, Denver, Salt Lake City, and Atlanta hubs. The airline's fleet of 282 aircraft includes (52) Embraer EMB 120 Brasilia, (140) Bombardier CRJ200, (13) CRJ700, (56) 3-class CRJ700, and (21) 2-class CRJ900 aircraft.

IATA: OO / 302   **Callsign**: "SKYWEST"   **ICAO**: SKW   skywest.com

CRJ-900 in a special paint scheme celebrating the airline's 35 year anniversary

TSA TRANS STATES AIRLINES

Founded in 1982 as Resort Air, Trans States Airlines began flying as AmericanConnection in December 2001 and operates today under the United Express and US Airways Express brand names with maintenance bases in St. Louis and Washington Dulles International Airport. The regional carrier operates at United Airlines' bases at IAD, ORD and DEN, and at PIT for US Airways. The St. Louis-based company is under ownership of Trans States Holdings, Inc. and operates a fleet of (9) Embraer EMB-145EP and (20) EMB-145LR aircraft. The airline changed its name from Resort Air to Trans States in 1989, and served as Trans World Express for mainline Trans World Airlines (TWA) until the legacy airline giant's assets were acquired by American Airlines in April, 2001.

IATA: AX / 414   **Callsign**: "WATERSKI"   **ICAO**: LOF   transstates.net

Embraer EMB-145LR

United Express • US Airways Express • US Airways Shuttle

UNITED EXPRESS

Bombardier CRJ-700

United Express is a brand name for United Airlines, Inc. in which several regional airlines operate commuter feeder flights for the Chicago-based airline, primarily connecting smaller cities and communities with United's domestic hub airports. The airlines that make up United Express are: Chautauqua Airlines, Colgan Air, GoJet Airlines, Mesa Airlines, Shuttle America, SkyWest Airlines, and Trans States Airlines. Many select United Express regional jet flights from United's five hubs at ORD, DEN, LAX, SFO, and IAD offer explus. These state-of-the-art aircraft come complete with larger overhead bins, more cabin space and leather seats throughout.

US AIRWAYS EXPRESS

Embraer EMB-175

US Airways Express is a brand name for US Airways in which several regional airlines operate commuter feeder flights for the Phoenix-based airline, primarily connecting smaller cities and communities with US Airways domestic hub airports. The airlines that make up US Airways Express are: Piedmont Airlines, PSA Airlines, (both wholly-owned by US Airways Group), Mesa Airlines, Chautauqua Airlines, Republic Airlines, Air Wisconsin, Cape Air, and Trans States Airlines.

US AIRWAYS *Shuttle*

Airbus A-320

US Airways Shuttle is the brand name used by US Airways to market its heavily-traveled, highly-competitive business routes between Boston, New York's La Guardia Airport, and Washington D.C.'s Regan National Airport. America's first Air-Shuttle was operated by Eastern Air Lines in 1961 and was in service until 1989 when it was purchased by real-estate developer and American business magnate Donald Trump, and operated Eastern Air Shuttle's Boeing 727 aircraft as The Trump Shuttle from 1989 to 1990. USAir Group acquired full ownership of the Shuttle and its routes by April 1992. With flights scheduled frequently on an hourly basis, US Airways Shuttle offers complimentary beer and wine, both first class and coach.

89

U.S. Airport Identifiers

Most airports providing airline service listed only.

A

Aberdeen, SD	ABR
Abilene, TX	ABI
Adak Island, AK	ADK
Akiachak, AK	KKI
Akiak, AK	AKI
Akron/Canton, OH	CAK
Akuton, AK	KQA
Alakanuk, AK	AUK
Alamogordo, NM	ALM
Alamosa, CO	ALS
Albany, NY	ALB
Albany, OR	CVO
Albuquerque, NM	ABQ
Aleknagik, AK	WKK
Alexandria, LA	AEX
Allakaket, AK	AET
Allentown, PA	ABE
Alliance, NE	AIA
Alpena, MI	APN
Altoona, PA	AOO
Amarillo, TX	AMA
Ambler, AK	ABL
Anaktueuk, AK	AKP
Anchorage, AK	ANC
Angoon, AK	AGN
Aniak, AK	ANI
Anvik, AK	ANV
Appleton, WI	ATW
Arcata, CA	ACV
Arctic Village, AK	ARC
Asheville, NC	AVL
Ashland, KY/Huntington, WV	HTS
Aspen, CO	ASE
Athens, GA	AHN
Atka, AK	AKB
Atlanta, GA	ATL
Atlantic City, NJ	ACY
Atqasuk, AK	ATK
Augusta, GA	AGS
Augusta, ME	AUG
Austin, TX	AUS

B

Bakersfield, CA	BFL
Baltimore, MD	BWI
Bangor, ME	BGR
Bar Harbour, ME	BHB
Barrow, AK	BRW
Barter Island, AK	BTI
Baton Rouge, LA	BTR
Bay City, MI	MBS
Beaumont/Port Arthur, TX	BPT
Beaver, AK	WBQ
Beckley, WV	BKW
Bedford, MA	BED
Belleville, IL	BLV
Bellingham, WA	BLI
Bemidji, MN	BJI
Benton Harbor, MI	BEH
Bethel, AK	BET
Bethlehem, PA	ABE
Bettles, AK	BTT
Billings, MT	BIL
Biloxi/Gulfport, MS	GPT
Binghamton, NY	BGM
Birch Creek, AK	KBC
Birmingham, AL	BHM
Bismarck, ND	BIS
Block Island, RI	BID
Bloomington, IL	BMI
Bluefield, WV	BLF
Boise, ID	BOI
Boston, MA	BOS
Boulder, CO	WBU
Boundary, AK	BYA
Bowling Green, KY	BWG
Bozeman, MT	BZN
Bradford, PA	BFD
Brainerd, MN	BRD
Brawnwood, TX	BWD
Bristol, VA	TRI
Brookings, SD	BKX
Brooks Lodge, AK	RBH
Brownsville, TX	BRO
Brunswick, GA	BQK
Buckland, AK	BKC
Buffalo, NY	BUF
Bullhead City/Laughlin, AZ	IFP
Burbank, CA	BUR
Burlington, IA	BRL
Burlington, VT	BTV
Butte, MT	BTM

C

Canton/Akron, OH	CAK
Cape Girardeau, MO	CGI
Cape Lisburne, AK	LUR
Cape Newenham, AK	EHM
Carbondale, IL	MDH
Carlsbad, CA	CLD
Carlsbad, NM	CNM
Carmel, CA	MRY
Casper, WY	CPR
Cedar City, UT	CDC
Cedar Rapids, IA	CID
Central, AK	CEM
Chadron, NE	CDR
Chalkyitsik, AK	CIK
Champaign/Urbana, IL	CMI
Charleston, SC	CHS
Charleston, WV	CRW
Charlotte, NC	CLT
Charlottesville, VA	CHO
Chattanooga, TN	CHA
Chefornak, AK	CYF
Chevak, AK	VAK
Cheyenne, WY	CYS
Chicago, IL - Midway	MDW
Chicago, IL - O'Hare	ORD
Chicken, AK	CKX
Chico, CA	CIC
Chignik, AK - Fisheries	KCG
Chignik, AK -	KCQ
Chignik, AK - Lagoon	KCL
Chisana, AK	CZN
Chisholm/Hibbing, MN	HIB
Chuathbaluk, AK	CHU
Cincinnati, OH	CVG
Circle Hot Springs, AK	CHP
Circle, AK	IRC
Clarks Point, AK	CLP
Clarksburg, WV	CKB
Clearwater/St Petersburg, FL	PIE
Cleveland, OH	CLE
Clovis, NM	CVN
Cody/Yellowstone, WY	COD
Coffee Point, AK	CFA
Coffman Cove, AK	KCC
Cold Bay, AK	CDB
College Station, TX	CLL
Colorado Springs, CO	COS
Columbia, MO	COU
Columbia, SC	CAE
Columbus, GA	CSG
Columbus, MS	GTR
Columbus, OH	CMH

90

U.S. Airport Identifiers

*Most airports providing airline service listed only.

Concord, CA	CCR
Concordia, KS	CNK
Cordova, AK	CDV
Corpus Christi, TX	CRP
Cortez, CO	CEZ
Craig, AK	CGA
Crescent City, CA	CEC
Crooked Creek, AK	CKO
Cube Cove, AK	CUW
Cumberland, MD	CBE
D	
Dallas, TX - Love Field	DAL
Dallas, TX - Dallas/Ft Worth Intl.	DFW
Dayton, OH	DAY
Daytona Beach, FL	DAB
Decatur, IL	DEC
Deering, AK	DRG
Del Rio, TX	DRT
Delta Junction, AK	DJN
Denver, CO – International	DEN
Des Moines, IA	DSM
Detroit, MI - Metro/Wayne County	DTW
Devil's Lake, ND	DVL
Dickinson, ND	DIK
Dillingham, AK	DLG
Dodge City, KS	DDC
Dothan, AL	DHN
Dubois, PA	DUJ
Dubuque, IA	DBQ
Duluth, MN	DLH
Durango, CO	DRO
Durham/Raleigh, NC	RDU
Dutch Harbor, AK	DUT
E	
Easton, PA	ABE
Eau Claire, WI	EAU
Edna Bay, AK	EDA
Eek, AK	EEK
Ekuk, AK	KKU
Ekwok, AK	KEK
El Centro, CA	IPL
El Dorado, AR	ELD
El Paso, TX	ELP
Elfin Cove, AK	ELV
Elim, AK	ELI
Elko, NV	EKO
Elmira, NY	ELM
Ely, MN	LYU

Emmonak, AK	EMK
Endicott, NY	BGM
Enid, OK	WDG
Erie, PA	ERI
Escanaba, MI	ESC
Eugene, OR	EUG
Eureka/Arcata, CA	ACV
Eureka, NV	EUE
Evansville, IN	EVV
F	
Fairbanks, AK	FAI
Fargo, ND	FAR
Farmington, NM	FMN
Fayetteville, AR - Municipal/Drake	FYV
Fayetteville, AR - Northwest Arkansas Regional	XNA
Fayetteville, NC	FAY
Flagstaff, AZ	FLG
Flint, MI	FNT
Florence, SC	FLO
Florence/Muscle Shoals/Sheffield, AL	MSL
Fort Collins/Loveland, CO	FNL
Fort Dodge, IA	FOD
Fort Lauderdale, FL	FLL
Fort Leonard Wood, MO	TBN
Fort Myers, FL	RSW
Fort Smith, AR	FSM
Fort Walton Beach, FL	VPS
Fort Wayne, IN	FWA
Fort Worth/Dallas, TX	DFW
Franklin, PA	FKL
Fresno, CA	FAT
G	
Gainesville, FL	GNV
Gallup, NM	GUP
Garden City, KS	GCK
Gary, IN	GYY
Gillette, WY	GCC
Glasgow, MT	GGW
Glendive, MT	GDV
Golovin, AK	GLV
Goodnews Bay, AK	GNU
Grand Canyon, AZ - National Park Airport	GCN
Grand Forks, ND	GFK
Grand Island, NE	GRI
Grand Junction, CO	GJT
Grand Rapids, MI	GRR

Grand Rapids, MN	GPZ
Grayling, AK	KGX
Great Falls, MT	GTF
Green Bay, WI	GRB
Greensboro/High Point/Winston-Salem, NC	GSO
Greenville, MS	GLH
Greenville, NC	PGV
Greenville/Spartanburg, SC	GSP
Groton/New London, CT	GON
Gulfport, MS	GPT
Gunnison/Crested Butte, CO	GUC
Gustavus, AK	GST
H	
Hagerstown, MD	HGR
Hailey/Ketchum/Sun Valley, ID	SUN
Haines, AK	HNS
Hampton, VA	PHF
Hana, HI - Island of Maui	HNM
Hanapepe, HI	PAK
Hancock, MI	CMX
Hanover, NH	LEB
Harlingen, TX	HRL
Harrisburg, PA	MDT
Harrison, AR	HRO
Hartford, CT	BDL
Havasupai, AZ	HAE
Havre, MT	HVR
Hayden, CO	HDN
Hays, KS	HYS
Healy Lake, AK	HKB
Helena, MT	HLN
Hendersonville, NC	AVL
Hibbing/Chisholm, MN	HIB
Hickory, NC	HKY
High Point/Greensboro, NC	GSO
Hilo, HI - Island of Hawaii	ITO
Hilton Head, SC	HHH
Hobbs, NM	HBB
Hollis, AK	HYL
Holy Cross, AK	HCR
Homer, AK	HOM
Honolulu, HI - Island of Oahu	HNL
Hoolehua, HI - Island of Molokai	MKK
Hoonah, AK	HNH
Hooper Bay, AK	HPB
Hot Springs, AR	HOT
Houston, TX - Hobby	HOU
Houston, TX - Intercontinental	IAH

91

U.S. Airport Identifiers

Most airports providing airline service listed only.

Hughes, AK	HUS
Huntington, WV/Ashland, KY	HTS
Huntsville, AL	HSV
Huron, SD	HON
Huslia, AK	HSL
Hyannis, MA	HYA
Hydaburg, AK	HYG

I

Idaho Falls, ID	IDA
Igiugig, AK	IGG
Iliamna, AK	ILI
Imperial, CA	IPL
Indianapolis, IN	IND
International Falls, MN	INL
Inyokern, CA	IYK
Iron Mountain, MI	IMT
Ironwood, MI	IWD
Islip, NY	ISP
Ithaca, NY	ITH

J

Jackson Hole, WY	JAC
Jackson, MS	JAN
Jackson, TN	MKL
Jacksonville, FL	JAX
Jacksonville, NC	OAJ
Jamestown, ND	JMS
Jamestown, NY	JHW
Janesville, WI	JVL
Johnson City, NY	BGM
Johnson City, TN	TRI
Johnstown, PA	JST
Jonesboro, AR	JBR
Joplin, MO	JLN
Juneau, AK	JNU

K

Kahului, HI - Island of Maui	OGG
Kake, AK	KAE
Kakhonak, AK	KNK
Kalamazoo, MI	AZO
Kalaupapa, HI - Island of Molokai	LUP
Kalskag, AK	KLG
Kaltag, AK	KAL
Kamuela, HI - Island of Hawaii	MUE
Kansas City, MO	MCI
Kapalua, HI - Island of Maui	JHM
Kasaan, AK	KXA

Kasigluk, AK	KUK
Kauai Island/Lihue, HI	LIH
Kearney, NE	EAR
Keene, NH	EEN
Kenai, AK	ENA
Ketchikan, AK	KTN
Key West, FL	EYW
Kiana, AK	IAN
Kilgore/Longview, TX	GGG
Killeen, TX	ILE
King Cove, AK	KVC
King Salmon, AK	AKN
Kingman, AZ	IGM
Kingsport, TN	TRI
Kipnuk, AK	KPN
Kirksville, MO	IRK
Kivalina, AK	KVL
Klamath Falls, OR	LMT
Klawock, AK	KLW
Knoxville, TN	TYS
Kobuk, AK	OBU
Kodiak, AK	ADQ
Kona, HI - Island of Hawaii	KOA
Kongiganak, AK	KKH
Kotlik, AK	KOT
Kotzebue, AK	OTZ
Koyukuk, AK	KYU
Kwethluk, AK	KWT
Kwigillingok, AK	KWK

L

La Crosse, WI	LSE
Lafayette, IN	LAF
Lafayette, LA	LFT
Lake Charles, LA	LCH
Lake Havasu City, AZ	HII
Lake Minchumina, AK	LMA
Lanai City, HI - Island of Lanai	LNY
Lancaster, PA	LNS
Lansing, MI	LAN
Laramie, WY	LAR
Laredo, TX	LRD
Las Vegas, NV	LAS
Latrobe, PA	LBE
Laurel, MS	PIB
Lawton/Ft. Sill, OK	LAW
Lebanon, NH	LEB
Levelock, AK	KLL
Lewisburg, WV	LWB

Lewiston, ID	LWS
Lewistown, MT	LWT
Lexington, KY	LEX
Liberal, KS	LBL
Lihue, HI - Island of Kaui	LIH
Lincoln, NE	LNK
Little Rock, AR	LIT
Long Beach, CA	LGB
Longview/Kilgore, TX	GGG
Lopez Island, WA	LPS
Los Angeles, CA	LAX
Louisville, KY	SDF
Loveland/Fort Collins, CO	FNL
Lubbock, TX	LBB

M

Macon, GA	MCN
Madison, WI	MSN
Madras, OR	MDJ
Manchester, NH	MHT
Manhattan, KS	MHK
Manistee, MI	MBL
Mankato, MN	MKT
Manley Hot Springs, AK	MLY
Manokotak, AK	KMO
Marietta, OH/Parkersburg, WV	PKB
Marion, IL	MWA
Marquette, MI	MQT
Marshall, AK	MLL
Martha's Vineyard, MA	MVY
Martinsburg, PA	AOO
Mason City, IA	MCW
Massena, NY	MSS
Maui, HI	OGG
Mcallen, TX	MFE
Mccook, NE	MCK
Mcgrath, AK	MCG
Medford, OR	MFR
Mekoryuk, AK	MYU
Melbourne, FL	MLB
Memphis, TN	MEM
Merced, CA	MCE
Meridian, MS	MEI
Metlakatla, AK	MTM
Meyers Chuck, AK	WMK
Miami, FL	MIA
Midland, MI	MBS
Midland/Odessa, TX	MAF
Miles City, MT	MLS

*Most airports providing airline service listed only.

U.S. Airport Identifiers

Milwaukee, WI	MKE
Minneapolis/St. Paul, MN	MSP
Minot, ND	MOT
Minto, AK	MNT
Mission, TX	MFE
Missoula, MT	MSO
Moab, UT	CNY
Mobile, AL	MOB
Modesto, CA	MOD
Moline, IL	MLI
Monroe, LA	MLU
Monterey, CA	MRY
Montgomery, AL	MGM
Montrose, CO	MTJ
Morgantown, WV	MGW
Moses Lake, WA	MWH
Mountain Home, AR	WMH
Mountain Village, AK	MOU
Muscle Shoals, AL	MSL
Muskegon, MI	MKG
Myrtle Beach, SC	MYR

N

Nantucket, MA	ACK
Napakiak, AK	WNA
Napaskiak, AK	PKA
Naples, FL	APF
Nashville, TN	BNA
Naukiti, AK	NKI
Nelson Lagoon, AK	NLG
New Chenega, AK	NCN
New Haven, CT	HVN
New Koliganek, AK	KGK
New London/Groton	GON
New Orleans, LA	MSY
New Stuyahok, AK	KNW
New York, NY - Kennedy	JFK
New York, NY - La Guardia	LGA
Newark, NJ	EWR
Newburgh/Stewart Field, NY	SWF
Newport News, VA	PHF
Newtok, AK	WWT
Nightmute, AK	NME
Nikolai, AK	NIB
Nikolski, AK	IKO
Noatak, AK	WTK
Nome, AK	OME
Nondalton, AK	NNL
Noorvik, AK	ORV

Norfolk, NE	OFK
Norfolk, VA	ORF
North Bend/Coos Bay, OR	OTH
North Platte, NE	LBF
Northway, AK	ORT
Nuiqsut, AK	NUI
Nulato, AK	NUL
Nunapitchuk, AK	NUP

O

Oakland, CA	OAK
Odessa/Midland, TX	MAF
Ogdensburg, NY	OGS
Oklahoma City, OK	OKC
Omaha, NE	OMA
Ontario, CA	ONT
Orange County, CA	SNA
Orlando, FL – Herndon Executive	ORL
Orlando, FL - International	MCO
Oshkosh, WI	OSH
Ottumwa, IA	OTM
Owensboro, KY	OWB
Oxnard/Ventura, CA	OXR

P

Paducah, KY	PAH
Page, AZ	PGA
Palm Springs, CA	PSP
Panama City, FL	PFN
Parkersburg, WV/Marietta, OH	PKB
Pasco/Richland/Kennewick, WA	PSC
Pedro Bay, AK	PDB
Pelican, AK	PEC
Pellston, MI	PLN
Pendleton, OR	PDT
Pensacola, FL	PNS
Peoria, IL	PIA
Perryville, AK	KPV
Petersburg, AK	PSG
Philadelphia, PA - International	PHL
Philadelphia, PA - Trenton/Mercer NJ	TTN
Phoenix, AZ	PHX
Pierre, SD	PIR
Pilot Point, AK - Ugashnik Bay	UGB
Pilot Point, AK	PIP
Pilot Station, AK	PQS
Pittsburgh, PA	PIT
Platinum, AK	PTU
Plattsburgh, NY	PLB
Pocatello, ID	PIH

Point Baker, AK	KPB
Point Hope, AK	PHO
Point Lay, AK	PIZ
Ponca City, OK	PNC
Ponce, Puerto Rico	PSE
Port Alsworth, AK	PTA
Port Angeles, WA	CLM
Port Arthur/Beaumont, TX	BPT
Port Clarence, AK	KPC
Port Heiden, AK	PTH
Port Moller, AK	PML
Port Protection, AK	PPV
Portage Creek, AK	PCA
Portland, ME	PWM
Portland, OR	PDX
Portsmouth, NH	PSM
Poughkeepsie, NY	POU
Prescott, AZ	PRC
Presque Isle, ME	PQI
Princeton, WV	BLF
Providence, RI	PVD
Provincetown, MA	PVC
Prudhoe Bay/Deadhorse, AK	SCC
Pueblo, CO	PUB
Pullman, WA	PUW

Q

Quincy, IL	UIN
Quinhagak, AK	KWN

R

Raleigh/Durham, NC	RDU
Rampart, AK	RMP
Rapid City, SD	RAP
Reading, PA	RDG
Red Devil, AK	RDV
Redding, CA	RDD
Redmond, OR	RDM
Reno, NV	RNO
Rhinelander, WI	RHI
Richmond, VA	RIC
Riverton, WY	RIW
Roanoke, VA	ROA
Roche Harbor, WA	RCE
Rochester, MN	RST
Rochester, NY	ROC
Rock Springs, WY	RKS
Rockford, IL	RFD
Rockland, ME	RKD
Rosario, WA	RSJ

93

U.S. Airport Identifiers

Most airports providing airline service listed only.

Roswell, NM	ROW
Ruby, AK	RBY
Russian Mission, AK	RSH
Rutland, VT	RUT
S	
Sacramento, CA	SMF
Saginaw/Midland bay, MI	MBS
Saint Cloud, MN	STC
Saint George Island, AK	STG
Saint George, UT	SGU
Saint Louis, MO	STL
Saint Mary's, AK	KSM
Saint Michael, AK	SMK
Saint Paul Island, AK	SNP
Salem, OR	SLE
Salina, KS	SLN
Salisbury-Ocean City, MD	SBY
Salt Lake City, UT	SLC
San Angelo, TX	SJT
San Antonio, TX	SAT
San Diego, CA	SAN
San Francisco, CA	SFO
San Jose, CA	SJC
San Juan, Puerto Rico	SJU
San Luis Obispo, CA	SBP
Sand Point, AK	SDP
Sanford, FL	SFB
Santa Ana, CA	SNA
Santa Barbara, CA	SBA
Santa Fe, NM	SAF
Santa Maria, CA	SMX
Santa Rosa, CA	STS
Saranac Lake, NY	SLK
Sarasota, FL	SRQ
Sault Ste Marie, MI	CIU
Savannah, GA	SAV
Savoonga, AK	SVA
Scammon Bay, AK	SCM
Scottsbluff, NE	BFF
Scranton/Wilkes Barre, PA	AVP
Seattle, WA – Lake Union/Kenmore Air Harbor	LKE
Seattle, WA - Seattle/Tacoma International	SEA
Selawik, AK	WLK
Seward, AK	SWD
Shageluk, AK	SHX
Shaktoolik, AK	SKK
Sheffield/Florence/Muscle Shoals, AL	MSL
Sheldon Point, AK	SXP

Sheridan, WY	SHR
Shishmaref, AK	SHH
Shreveport, LA	SHV
Shungnak, AK	SHG
Silver City, NM	SVC
Sioux City, IA	SUX
Sioux Falls, SD	FSD
Sitka, AK	SIT
Skagway, AK	SGY
Sleetmore, AK	SLQ
South Bend, IN	SBN
South Naknek, AK	WSN
Sothern Pines, NC	SOP
Spartanburg/Greenville, SC	GSP
Spokane, WA	GEG
Springfield, IL	SPI
Springfield, MO	SGF
St Petersburg/Clearwater, FL	PIE
State College/University Park, PA	SCE
Staunton, VA	SHD
Steamboat Springs, CO	SBS
Stebbins, AK	WBB
Stevens Point/Wausau, WI	CWA
Stevens Village, AK	SVS
Stewart Field/Newburgh, NY	SWF
Stockton, CA	SCK
Stony River, AK	SRV
Sun Valley/Haley/Ketchum, ID	SUN
Syracuse, NY	SYR
T	
Takotna, AK	TCT
Talkeetna, AK	TKA
Tallahassee, FL	TLH
Tampa, FL	TPA
Tanana, AK	TAL
Taos, NM	TSM
Tatitlek, AK	TEK
Teller Mission, AK	KTS
Telluride, CO	TEX
Tenakee Springs, AK	TKE
Terre Haute, IN	HUF
Tetlin, AK	TEH
Texarkana, AR	TXK
Thief River Falls, MN	TVF
Thorne Bay, AK	KTB
Tin City, AK	TNC
Togiak Village, AK	TOG
Tok, AK	TKJ

Toksook Bay, AK	OOK
Toledo, OH	TOL
Topeka, KS	FOE
Traverse City, MI	TVC
Trenton/Mercer, NJ	TTN
Tucson, AZ	TUS
Tulsa, OK	TUL
Tuluksak, AK	TLT
Tuntutuliak, AK	WTL
Tununak, AK	TNK
Tupelo, MS	TUP
Tuscaloosa, AL	TCL
Twin Falls, ID	TWF
Twin Hills, AK	TWA
Tyler, TX	TYR
U	
Unalakleet, AK	UNK
Urbana/Champaign, IL	CMI
Utica, NY	UCA
Utopia Creek, AK	UTO
V	
Vail / Eagle County, CO	EGE
Valdez, AK	VDZ
Valdosta, GA	VLD
Valparaiso, FL	VPS
Venetie, AK	VEE
Ventura/Oxnard, CA	OXR
Vernal, UT	VEL
Victoria, TX	VCT
Visalia, CA	VIS
W	
Waco, TX	ACT
Wainwright, AK	AIN
Wales, AK	WAA
Walla Walla, WA	ALW
Washington DC – Dulles	IAD
Washington DC – National	DCA
Waterfall, AK	KWF
Waterloo, IA	ALO
Watertown, NY	ART
Watertown, SD	ATY
Wausau/Stevens Point, WI	CWA
Wenatchee, WA	EAT
West Palm Beach, FL	PBI
West Yellowstone, MT	WYS
Westchester County, NY	HPN
Westerly, RI	WST

94

Most airports providing airline service listed only.

U.S. AIRPORT IDENTIFIERS

Westsound, WA	WSX
Whale Pass, AK	WWP
White Mountain, AK	WMO
White River, VT	LEB
Wichita Falls, TX	SPS
Wichita, KS	ICT
Wilkes Barre/Scranton, PA	AVP
Williamsburg/Newport News, VA	PHF
Williamsport, PA	IPT
Williston, ND	ISN
Wilmington, NC	ILM
Windsor Locks-Hartford,CT/Springfield, MA	BDL
Worcester, MA	ORH
Worland, WY	WRL
Wrangell, AK	WRG
Y	
Yakima, WA	YKM
Yakutat, AK	YAK
Yellowstone/Cody, WY	COD
Youngstown, OH	YNG
Yuma, AZ	YUM

Background photo: *Elrey Jeppesen Terminal*
Denver International Airport

Located in the extreme northeastern region and 25 miles from downtown Denver, Colorado, **Denver International Airport** (commonly referred to as DIA), is by far the **largest international airport in the United States by land size** with an area covering **53 square miles**, and the second largest international airport in the world. On average, some 1,700 flights depart and arrive here each day—through 95 gates and three concourses— accommodating more than 136,600 passengers daily, with approximately **fifty million passengers each year**. In 2007, approximately 43 percent of passengers flying into DIA connected onto other flights. Denver International Airport is home to low-cost carrier **Frontier Airlines**, and is **United Airlines' second largest hub** where it operates as the dominant carrier. DIA also serves as a focus city for Dallas-based **Southwest Airlines**. Since commencing service to Denver in January 2006, Southwest has added over 30 destinations, making Denver its fastest-growing market. The airport was reopened on February 28, 1995, replacing the former Denver Stapleton International Airport, and is globally recognized for its signature roofline, aesthetically designed to be reminiscent of the snow-capped **Rocky Mountains** in the winter. Runway 16R/34L is the **longest public-use runway in the nation, with a length of 16,000 feet**, which is over three miles long. The airport's elevation is **5,431 feet**, just over one mile, above sea level; hence the City of Denver's time-honored nickname, **"Mile-High City"**.

PHOTO COURTESY OF DENVER INTERNATIONAL AIRPORT

INDEX

A + Rewards, 7, **8**, 9, 31
AAdvantage, **20**, 21
AMR Corp., 19, 21, 76
AMResorts, 67
ATR Regional Aircraft (ATR)
    ATR-42: 77, 79
    ATR-72: 76
"Acey" *(callsign)*, 77
Admirals Club, **20**, 21
Air California (AirCal), 20
AirFairs, **32**
Air France, 12
Air Line Pilots Association, (ALPA), 59
"Air Shuttle" *(callsign)*, 82, 85
Air Southwest, 47, 49
AirTran Airlines (former), 7, 8
AirTran Airways, **6-9**, 31
AirTran Corporation, 7
AirTran Holdings, 8,9
Air Wisconsin Airlines Corp., 64, **76**, 89
Airbus S.A.S., 31, 51
Airbus: *aircraft index:*
    A300: 19, 23
    A318: 31, 33
    A319: 29, **30**, 31, 33, **50**, 51, **53**, 61, 65, 71, 73
    A320: 29, 31, **33**, **38**, 39, **41**, 60, 61, **65**, **66**, 67, **68-70**, 71, **73**, **89**
    A321: 51, 53, 65
    A330: 29, 36, 37, **62**, 65
    A350: 36, 37
Airways, Inc., 8
Airways Corporation, 7
Alaska Air Group, 11, 84

Alaska Airlines, **1**, **10**, 11, 12, **13**, 81, 84
Alaska Airlines Magazine, 13
Alaska Airlines Partnerships, 80
Alaska Star Airlines, 11
Albuquerque International Sunport, NM (ABQ), 83
Ali'i Club, 86
Ali'i Rewards, 86
All American Airways, 63
All American Aviation Co., 63, 65
Allegheny Airlines, 63
Allegheny Commuter, 63, 87
Allegiant Air, **14**, 15, **16**, **17**
Allegiant Information Systems, 17
Allegiant Travel Co., 15
Allegiant Vacations, 17
Aloha Air Group, 84
Aloha Airlines, 35, 84
Aloha Island Air, 84
America West Airlines, 64, **65**, 81
America West Express, 81
American Airlines, 12, **18-21**, 35, 77, 88
American Airways, 19, 21
AmericanConnection, 21, **76**, 77, 88
American Eagle Airlines, 19, 21, **76**
American Trans Air (ATA), 35
American Way Magazine, 21
Amstar Destination Management, 67
Apollo Reservation System, 61
Apple Leisure Group, 67
Apple Vacations, 67
Arizona One, 47
Atlanta Journal-Constitution, 7
Atlantic Southeast Airlines (ASA), 28, **77**, 80

Attaché Magazine, 65
Aviation Corporation, The, 19
Awards and accolades, 7, 24, 32, 40, 43, 72

Baltimore/Washington Int'l Airport, MD (BWI), 9, 68
Bankruptcy, Chapter Eleven, 55, 60, 64
Bar Harbor Airlines, 81
Barnes, Leslie O., 63
Barnstable Municipal Airport, MA (HYA), 77
Beech Craft Co., 63
Beechcraft, *See Hawker Beechcraft Corp.*
Bellingham Int'l Airport, WA (BLI), 15
Best Care Club, **44**, 45
Best Care Cuisine, 43
Blue 100, 39
"Blue Streak" *(callsign)*, 87
Blue Suede Shoes (JetBlue Airways), 39
Board Room, **12**, 13
Boeing: *aircraft index:*
    B80-A: 59
    B707: 19, 23
    B717: **6**,-9, 35, 36, **37**, **42**, 43, **45**
    B727: 19, 27, 55, 64, 89
    B737: 7, 8, **9**, **10**, 12, **13**, 21, **25**, 27-29, 31, **46**, 47, **48**, **49**, **54**, **56**, **57**, 60, 61, 63, 64, 65
    B747: **29**, 61
    B757: 21, **25**, 28, **29**, **61**, 65
    B767: **18**, 21, 25, 27, 29, **34**, 35, 36, **37**, 64, 65
    B777: **21**, **22**, 25, **26**, 29, **58**, **61**
    B787: 21, 25
Boeing Air Transport, 59

INDEX

Boeing customer codes: (**codes** in bold)
    2A: 37, **22**: 61, **23**: 21, **24**: 25, **32**: 29,
    90: 13, **B7**: 65, **BD**: 9, **BL**: 45, **H4**: 49
Bombardier *aircraft index:*
    Dash 8 Q100: **80**, **82**, 84, 86
    Dash 8 Q200: **76**, **78**, 79
    Dash 8 Q300: 88
    Dash 8 Q400: 31, 33, **78**, 79, **84**, **104**
    DH-4: 19
    DH-8: **84**, **86**
Bombardier Canadair *aircraft index:*
    CRJ100: 29, 78
    CRJ200: 29, **76**, 77, **79**, **82**, **85**, **87**, 88
    CRJ700: 29, **76**, 77, **82**, 84, 85, 87-**89**
    CRJ900: 29, **77**, **78**, **80**, 85, **88**
Brand Spankin' Blue (JetBlue Airways), 39
Braniff International Airlines, 47, 55
Branson, Sir Richard, 71
Brendan Airways, LLC, 68, 69
"Brick Yard" *(callsign)*, 87
British Aerospace, 63
    BAe Jetstream 31, 87
British Aircraft Corp. *aircraft index:*
    BAC 111, 63
British Airways, 12
Britt Airways, 81
BusinessFirst, **24**
Boll weevil, *insect*, 27

"C Air" *(callsign)*, 77
CMS (Reservations system), 29
"Cactus" *(callsign)*, 65
California One, 47
Canadair, *See Bombardier*

Cape Air, **77**, 79, 89
Capital Air Lines, 59
Cathay Pacific Airways, 12
Celebrated Living Magazine, 21
Cessna Aircraft Company: *aircraft index:*
    180: 83
    206: 83
    207: 83
    208-B: 83, 86
    402-C: **77**, 79, 87
    F-406: 83
Champlain Enterprises, Inc., 78
Charter One, 51,53
Chase Capital Corp., 39
Chautauqua Airlines, 28, 64, 76, **77**, 79, 80, 85, 89
Chicago And Southern Airlines, 27
China, Peoples Republic of, 60
Church, Ellen, 59
"Citrus" *(callsign)*, 9
Civil Reserve Air Fleet (CRAF), 55
Colgan Air, 64, **78**, 79, 89
"Colorado the Ram", **33**
Comair, 28, 29, **78**, 80
CommutAir, **78**, 79
Compass Airlines, 28, 29, **79**, 80
"Compass Rose" *(callsign)*, 79
Condé Nast Traveler, 40, 43, 56, 67, 72
Conquest Sun Airlines, 7,9
Continental Airlines, 12, **22-25**, 31, 35, 77, 78, 79, 81
Continental Connection, 24, 25, 77, **78**, **79**, 83
Continental Express, 24, 25, 77, **79**

Continental magazine, **24**, 25
Continental Micronesia, 24, 25
Convair: *aircraft index:*
    240: 23
    340: 23
    550: 63
    880: 11
Crown Room Club, 29
Cuddeback, Leon, 59
Curtiss Aeroplane And Motor Co. (1916)
    Curtiss Condor: 19
Customer Bill of Rights, **40**

Dallas/Ft. Worth Int'l Airport, TX (DFW), 19, 21
Dallas Love Field, TX (DAL), 47-49
Delta Air Corp., 27, 29
Delta Air Lines, 7, 12, **26-29**, 60, 77-80, 81, 85
Delta Air Service, 29
Delta Connection, 28, 29, 77, 78, **80**, **81**, 85, **87**, 88
Delta Express, 28
Delta Heritage Museum, 28
Delta Shuttle, 29, **80**
Denver Int'l Airport, CO (DEN), 3, 24, 82, 83, 92, 93, **95**
Denver Stapleton Airport (closed), 23, 31
Department of Defense, U.S. (DOD), 15
Deregulation, 11, 23, 28
    Act of 1978, 63
Desert Storm, Operation, 55
DIRECTV, 39
Dividend Miles, 65
Douglas Aircraft Co.: *See McDonnell-Douglas, Boeing*

INDEX

Douglas Int'l Airport, NC (CLT), 64, 87
Dulles International Airport, VA (IAD), 60, 61, 71, 82, 85, 88
"De-bundling", 3
De Havilland Aircraft Co., *See Bombardier*

EZR (Reservations System), 25
"Eagle Flight" *(callsign)*, 76
EarlyReturns, 8, 31, **32**, 33
Eastern Air Lines, 7, 20, 23, 89
Eastern Air Shuttle, 89
Elevate, **72**, 73
Embraer, 81, 85
Embraer, *aircraft index:*
    135: 43, 45, 76, 85
    140: **76**
    145: 43, 45, 76, **81**, 85, **88**
    170: 43, 45, **77**, **85**, **86**, 87, **88**
    175: 29, **79**, 80, **87**, 88, **89**
    190: 39, 40, **41**
    1200ER Brasilia: 83, 88
Empire Airlines, 63
Employee Stock Ownership Plan (ESOP), 59
Entrepreneur magazine, 7
Era Aviation, 12, **80**, 81
Executive Airlines, 76
Express Airlines One, 87
ExpressJet Airlines, 79, **81**
explus, 82, 89

FAA Diamond Award, 32, 43
Fairchild Aircraft: *aircraft index:*
    SA227-DC: 86
Federal Aviation Administration (FAA), 43

"Flagship" *(callsign)*, 87
"Flip the Bottlenose Dolphin", 31
"Flying W", 27
Fokker, *aircraft index:*
    F-28: 63
    F-100: 64
Fort Collins-Loveland Municipal Airport, CO (FNL), 16, **17**
Fort Lauderdale-Hollywood Int'l Airport, FL (FLL), **4**, 15, 83
FORTUNE magazine, 24
Franklin, William, 47
Freddie Awards, 43, 44
Free Spirit, **52**, 53
Freedom Airlines, 28, 80, **81**, 85
"Frontier Air" *(callsign)*, 81
Frontier Airlines (former), 23, 31
Frontier Airlines (current), 8, 12, **30-33**, 60, 84
Frontier Alaska, **81**
Frontier Alaska Company, 80, 83
"Frontier Flight" *(callsign)*, 33
Frontier Flying Service, 80, 81
Frontier Holdings, Inc., 33
First Flight Certificates, 67
"Fog buster", 11

Gallagher, Maurice J., 15, **16**
Gavarnie Holding, LLC, 84
General Mitchell Int'l Airport, WI (MKE), 43, 44, 83, 85, 87
Georgia 100, 7
"Getaway" *(callsign)*, 69
"Ginger the red fox pup", 84
go!, **82**

go! Express, **82**
GoJet Airlines, **82**, 89
GoldPlus, 36
Gold Carpet Service, 23
Golden Nugget Service, 11
GO Magazine, 9
Great Lakes Airlines, **83**
Green, T.F. Int'l Airport, RI (PVD), 51
Grizwald's Gourmet Cafe, 32
"Grizwald the Grizzly Bear", **32**
"Gulf Flight" *(callsign)*, 83
Gulfstream International Airlines, 79, **83**

Hageland Aviation Services, 80, 81, **83**
Hana Hou! magazine, **36**, 37
"Hank the Bobcat", **32**, 33
Hanscom Field, MA (BED), 88
Harrah's Entertainment, Inc., 15
Harrison, Ponder, 15
Hart, Jess E., 23
Hartsfield-Jackson Atlanta Int'l Airport, GA (ATL), **3**, 7, 8, 27
Hawaii Island Air, *See Island Air*
Hawaiian Airlines, **34-37**
Hawaiian Holdings, Inc., 37
HawaiianMiles, **36**, 37
Hawker Beechcraft, *aircraft index:*
    Beech 99: 63
    Beech 1900D: **79**, 80, **83**
    Beech 1900C: **81**, **83**
"Hector the Sea Otter", 31, **32**
Hemispheres magazine, 61
Henson Airlines, 63, 86
Hewlitt Packard, 39

Index

HoTH's Air Group Holdings, 81
Honolulu Int'l Airport, HI (HNL), 36
Hopkins Int'l Airport, OH (CLE), 23, 78
Horizon Air, 11, **12**, 13, **84**
Huff Daland Dusters, 27
Hyannis Air Service, 77

I (heart) blue, **38**
IATA accounting numbers, *index:*
   001, 21; **005**, 25; **003**, 79; **006**, 29; **016**, 61;
   027, 13; **037**, 65; **052**, 87; **173**, 37; **268**, 17;
   279, 41; **302**, 88; **303**, 76; **306**, 77; **332**, 9;
   336, 69; **337**, 57; **339**, 86; **347**, 84; **363**, 77;
   414, 88; **415**, 86; **422**, 33; **426**, 78; **430**, 87;
   449, 83; **453**, 45; **477**, 81; **481**, 84; **487**, 53;
   517, 81; **526**, 49; **533**, 85; **573**, 82; **582**, 85;
   808, 80; **841**, 78; **846**, 83; **862**, 77; **886**, 78;
   919, 88; **984**, 73
IATA designators, *index:*
   3M, 83; **7H**, 80; **9E**, 87; **9K**, 77; **9L**, 78;
   AA, 21; **AS**, 13; **AX**, 88; **B6**, 41; **C5**, 78;
   CO, 25; **CP**, 79; **DL**, 29; **EV**, 77; **F8**, 81;
   F9, 33; **FL**, 9; **G4**, 17; **G7**, 87; **83**; **HA**, 37;
   KS, 86; **L4**, 84; **MQ**, 76; **MW**, 86; **NK**, 53;
   OH, 78; **OO**, 88; **QX**, 84; **RP**, 76, 77;
   RW, 87; **S5**, 88; **SY**, 57; **U5**, 69; **UA**, 61;
   US, 65, 86, 87; **VX**, 73; **WN**, 49; **WP**, 82,
   84; **XE**, 81; **XJ**, 85; **YV**, 82, 85; **YX**, 45;
   ZF, 81; **ZK**, 83; **ZW**, 76
ICAO designators, *index:*
   AAL, 21; **AAY**, 17; **ASA**, 13; **ASH**, 82, 85;
   ASQ, 77; **AWE**, 65; **AWI**, 76; **BTA**, 81;
   BUG, 86; **CAL**, 25; **CHQ**, 76, 77; **CJC**, 78;
   COM, 78; **CPZ**, 79; **DAL**, 29; **EGF**, 76;
   ERH, 80; **FFT**, 33; **FLG**, 87; **FRL**, 81;
   FTA, 81; **GFT**, 83; **GJS**, 82; **GLA**, 83;
   GWY, 69; **HAG**, 83; **HAL**, 37; **JBU**, 41;
   JIA, 87; **KAP**, 77; **LOF**, 88; **MEP**, 45;
   MES, 85; **MKU**, 82, 84; **NKS**, 53;
   PDT, 86; **PEN**, 86; **QXE**, 84; **RPA**, 87;
   SCX, 57; **SKW**, 88; **SSX**, 84; **SWA**, 49;
   TCF, 88; **TRS**, 9; **UAL**, 61; **UCA**, 78;
   VRD, 73
Iflygo magazine, 82
Illinois One, 47
In-flight Entertainment System (IFE), 71
Inside Flyer magazine, 44
Inter-Island Airways, LTD, 35, 37
International Association of Machinists, 59
Island Air, 82, **84**

J.D. Power and Associates, 40
Jeppessen, Elrey (airport terminal), **95**
Jet America Airlines, 11
JetBlue Airways, **38-41**
"Jet Link" *(callsign)*, 81
Jetstream International Airlines, 87
John F. Kennedy Int'l Airport, NY (JFK), 39,
   40, 41, 71, 78, 81
   Terminal 5 ("T5"), 40
John Wayne Airport, CA (SNA), 71

K-C Aviation, 43
KLM Royal Dutch Airlines, 12
Kahului Airport, Maui, HI (OGG), 36
Kansas City Int'l Airport, MO (MCI), 83
Kelleher, Herbert D., 47
Kelley, Doug, 55

Kimberly-Clark Corp., 43
King, Rollin, 47
Korean Air, 12
LA/Ontario Int'l Airport, 83
LAN Chilean Airlines, 12
La Guardia Airport, NY (LGA), 78, 80, 88, 89
Lake Central Airlines, 63
"Lakes Air" *(callsign)*, 83
Lambert Field, MO (STL), 76, 83
"Larry the Lynx", 32, **33**
Levy, Andrew, 15
Liberty Int'l Airport, NJ (EWR), 78, 81
"Lindbergh" *(callsign)*, 82
Lindbergh, Charles A., 19
LiveTV, 31
Lockheed Martin, *aircraft index:*
   L-1011 TriStar, 35
Logan Int'l Airport, MA (BOS), 78, 80, 88
Logan Int'l Airport, MT (BIL), 83
"Lola and Max", **33**
Lone Star One, 47
Los Angeles Int'l Airport, CA (LAX), 15
Lufthansa German Airlines, 39
"Luke the Lynx Kitten", **84**
Lynx Aviation, 31-33, **84**

MLT Vacations, 55
MN Airlines, LLC, 57
Maintenance Operations Center (UA), 59
Maryland One, 47, **48**
McCarran Int'l Airport, NV (LAS), 15, 48, **49**
McDonnell-Douglas, 7, 63, *aircraft index:*
   DC-3, 19, 23, 35, 59
   DC-4, 11

INDEX

McDonnell-Douglas aircraft index (cont'd)
  DC-6, 19
  DC-8, 35,59
  DC-9, 7, 8, 15, 29, 35, 43, 63
  DC-10, 19, 23, 27, 55
  MD-80, 15, 31, 43
  MD-81, 43
  MD-82, 12, 17, 43, **104**
  MD-83, 12, **14**, 17, 21
  MD-88, **17**, 29, 43, **81**
  MD-87, 17
  MD-90, 29
  MD-95 (B717), 7
McGee, Linious, 11
McGee Airways, 11, 13
Mendota Heights, City of, MN, 55, 57
"Mercury" *(callsign)*, 88
Mesa Air Group, 82, 85
Mesa Airlines, 64, 82, **85**, 89
Mesaba Airlines,
Mesaba Aviation, 85
Metropolitan Wayne County Int'l Airport, MI (DTW), 52
Miami Int'l Airport, FL (MIA), 20, 83
"Midex" *(callsign)*, 45
Midway Airport, IL (MDW), 47, 59
Midwest Air Group, 43
Midwest Airlines, **42-45**, 85
Midwest Class, 43, **44**
Midwest Connect, 43, 45, 77, **85**, 87
Midwest Express Airlines, 43, 45
Midwest Miles, 43, **44**, 45
Mileage Plan, **12**, 13
Mileage Plus, 59, **60**, 61

Minneapolis/St. Paul Int'l Airport, MN (MSP), 79, 82, 85
  Humphrey Terminal, 56 Mohawk Airlines, 63
"Moku" *(callsign)*, 82, 84
Mokulele Airlines, 12, **86**, 88
Mokulele Express, 86
Mood lighting (cabin), 71, **72**
Morris Air, 47
Muse, Lamar, 47
Muse Air, 47
My Midwest magazine, 45

Nantucket Airlines, 77
National Air Transport, 59
National Association of Securities Dealers Automated Quotations (NASDAQ), 7,15
  Index of ticker symbols: **ALGT**: 17,
  HA: 37, **JBLU**: 41, **RJET**: 45, **UAUA**: 61
National Basketball Association, 47
Neeleman, David, 39
Nevada One, 47
New Air, 39
New Mexico One, 47
New York Air, 23
New York Stock Exchange (NYSE), 9, 64
  Index of ticker symbols:
  AAI: 9, **ALK**: 13, **AMR**: 21, **CAL**: 25,
  DAL: 29, **LCC**: 64, 65, **LUV**: 49
Newton Square, City of, PA, 67, 69
Nexos magazine, 21
Nine Dollar Fare Club, **52**
Northeast Airlines, 27
Northern Bites, 12
Northwest Airlines, 27, 29, 55, 85, 87

Northwest Airlink, 7, 79, 85, 87
Northwest Orient, 85
Nuts About Southwest
  corporate blog, 48

O'Hare International Airport, IL (ORD), 19, 21, 59, 61, 82, 85
Olson, Captain Jim, 55
Olson, Joan Smith, 55
OnePass, 23, 25, 79
oneworld, 21, 76
Open Skies, 39
Orlando Int'l Airport, FL (MCO), 28
Orlando Sanford Int'l Airport (SFB), 15

PSA Airlines (current), 64, 65, **87**, 89
Pacific Air Transport, 59
Pacific Southwest Airlines (PSA), 63, 64, 87
Paine Field, WA (PAE), 11
Palm Beach Int'l Airport, FL (PBI), 83
Pan Am Shuttle, 27, 80
Pan American World Airways (Pan Am), 27
Panasonic Aviation, 71
"Peninsula" *(callsign)*, 86
Peninsula Airways (PenAir), 12, **86**
PEOPLExpress Airlines, 23, 31
Petters Aviation, LLC, 55
Phoenix-Mesa Gateway Airport, AZ (AZA), 15, 16
Picnic Packs, 12
Piedmont Airlines (former), 63-65, 86, 87
Piedmont Airlines (current), 63-65, **86**, 89
Pinnacle Airlines, 28, 78, 80, **87**
Pioneer Airlines, 23

101

Index

Piper Aircraft, Inc.
    PA-31, 81
Preferred Perks, 67, **68**, 69
Premier Club, **36**, 37
Presidents Club, **24**, 25
Princeville Airways, 84
Project 767, 27
Provincetown-Boston Airlines (PBA), 81
Pualani, **36**

Qantas Airways, 12
qwerty (keyboard), 71

Rapid Rewards, **48**, 49
Reciprocal earning, meaning of, 8
Regan National Airport, VA (DCA), 8, 51, 63, 78, 80, 89
Red (IFE system), 71
Red Carpet Club, **60**, 61
"Redwood" *(callsign)*, 73
Republic Airlines (former), 85, 87
Republic Airlines (current), 43, 64, 85, **87**, 89
Republic Airways Holdings, 32, 33, 45, 77, 86-88
Resort Air, 88
Roam magazine, 69
Robertson Aircraft Corp., 19
Rocky Mountain Air, 81

SAGE system, U.S. Gov't, 19
Saab Aircraft, *Index of aircraft:*
    340: 29, 78, 79, **85**, 87
San Francisco Int'l Airport, CA (SFO), 59, 71
Saver Seats, 43
Seattle-Tacoma Int'l Airport, WA (SEA), 13, 71

Semi-Automated Business Research Environment (SABRE), 13, 19, 21, 33, 37, 41, 45, 49, 57
Senior fares, induction of, 48
September 11, 2001 tradgedies, 43, 55
Sahmu, 47
SHARES *(reservations system)*, 65
Share the Spirit, community program, 48
"Shasta" *(callsign)*, 84
Shuttle America, 28, 80, 86, **88**, 89
Shuttle by United, 60
Signature Seats, 43, **44**
Signature Service, 43
Sikorsky Aircraft Corp., *index of aircraft:*
    S-38, 35
    S-43, 35
Silver One, 47
Six, Robert F., 23
Sky Club, **28**, 29
Sky Harbor Int'l Airport, AZ (PHX), 64, 81, 83
Sky Lounge, 59
Sky magazine, 29
SkyMiles, **28**, 29
Sky Picnic, 67
Sky Sleeper, 19
SkySpeed *(reservations system)*, 9, 53
SkyTeam, 29, 79, 80
SkyTrax, 40
SkyWest, Inc., 88
SkyWest Airlines, 28, 77, 80, **88**, 89
Skylights magazine, **52**, 53
Skyway Airlines, 43, 45
Slam Dunk One, 47
Smith, C.R., 20

Song, 28
Soros, George, 39
Southern Airways, 7
southwest.com, 48
Southwest Airlines, 39, **46-49**, 60
"Speedbuggy" *(callsign)*, 86
Spirit Airlines, **50-53**
Spirit magazine, 47
"Spirit Wings" *(callsign)*, 53
Spirit of Delta, 27
St. Petersburg-Clearwater Int'l Airport, FL (PIE), 15
Star Air Service, 11
Star Alliance, 59, 61, 65
Starliner 75, **12**
Stinson Aircraft Company, 11
    Reliant SR-10, 63
Sun Country Airlines, **54**, 55, **56**, 57
Sun Country magazine, 57
Sunseeker magazine, 17
Super 80, **21**
SystemOne, 23

Tampa Int'l Airport, FL (TPA), 83
Ted, 59
Ted Stevens Anchorage Int'l Airport, AK (ANC), 80, 86
Texas Air Corp., 23
Ticketless travel, induction of, 48
TPG Capital, 43, 45
Trans-Caribbean Airways, 19
Trans States Airlines, 64, **88**, 89
Trans States Holdings, 82, 88
Trans World Airlines (TWA), 8, 20, 88

INDEX

Trans World Express, 88
Travel+Leisure magazine, 43, 56, 67
Triple Crown One, 47
TrueBlue, **40**, 41
Trump, Donald, 89
Trump Shuttle, 89
Tulip, 59

UAL Corp., 60, 61
Udi's Handcrafted Foods, 32
Ufly Plus, **56**
Ufly Rewards, **56**, 57
ULCC, 52
United Airlines, 23, 31, **58-61**, 77, 82, 88, 89
United Express, 60, 61, 76-78, 82, 85, **88**, **89**
United States Air Force, 55
USA3000 Airlines, **66**, 67, **68**, **69**
USAir, 63, 64, 86, 87
USAir Group, 89
US Airways, **62-65**, 77, 87-89
US Airways Club, **64**, 65
US Airways Express, 63-65, **76**, 77, 78, 85, 86, **87**, 88, **89**
US Airways Group, 65, 86, 87
US Airways magazine, 65
US Airways Shuttle, 65, **89**
U.S. EPA Climate Leaders Program, 72

VAI Partners, LLC, 71
ValuJet Airlines, 7, 8
Vee Neal Airlines, 87
Varney, Walter T., 23
Varney Air Lines, 59, 61
Varney Speed Lines, 23, 25

Virgin America, **70**, 71, **72**, **73**
Virgin Atlantic Airways, 71
Virgin Blue, 71
Virgin Galactic, 71
Virgin Group, LTD., 71
Virgin Nigeria, 71

Wally the Gray Wolf, **30**
Wayne County Airport, MI (DTW), **68**
"Waterski" *(callsign)*, 88
Western Airlines, 3, 27
WestJet (Canada), 39
Weston Presido Capital, 39
Whitebox Advisors, 55
Wi-fi, 8, 12
Widget, **26**, 28, **29**
Wild Blue Yonder Magazine, 33
Wiley Post-Will Rogers Memorial Airport, AK (BRW), 83
William B. Hobby Airport, TX (HOU), 48
Winglet, blended, 48
Woolman, C.E., 27
WorldClubs, 28
WorldPerks, 28
World War II, 31

XM Satellite Radio, 8, 39

yellowbirds, 27

Zagat airline survey, 43

103

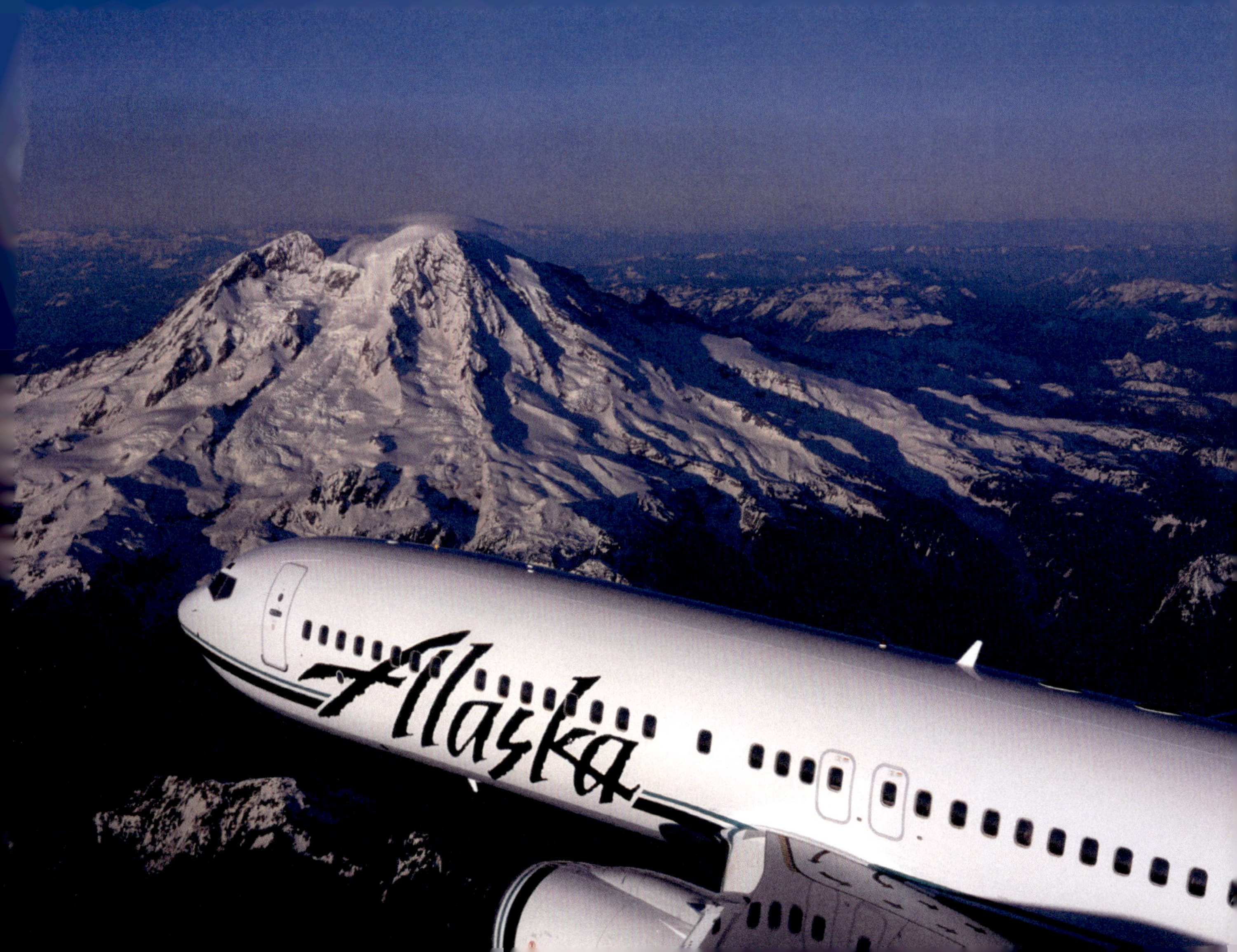
Alaska

Made in the USA
Middletown, DE
30 October 2018